THE WORDS OF
PEACE

THE WORDS OF
PEACE

SELECTIONS FROM THE SPEECHES OF THE WINNERS OF THE NOBEL PEACE PRIZE

FOURTH EDITION

SELECTED AND EDITED BY
IRWIN ABRAMS

Foreword by
President Jimmy Carter

Newmarket Press
New York

The Newmarket "Words Of" Series

FOURTH EDITION

10 9 8 7 6 5 4 3 2 1

Library of Congress Cataloging-in-Publication Data

The words of peace : selections from the speeches of the winners of the Nobel Peace Prize / selected and edited by Irwin Abrams ; foreword by President Jimmy Carter. -- 4th ed.
    p. cm.
"Published simultaneously in the United States of America and in Canada."
Includes bibliographical references and index.
ISBN 978-1-55704-786-1 (pb : alk. paper) 1. Peace. 2. Peace--Awards. 3. Nobel Prizes. 4. Nobel Prize winners. I. Abrams, Irwin
JZ5538.W76 2008
327.1'72--dc22

                                        2008008748

ISBN: 978-1-55704-786-1 (paperback)
ISBN: 978-1-55704-809-7 (hardcover)

QUANTITY PURCHASES

Companies, professional groups, clubs, and other organizations may qualify for special terms when ordering quantities of this title. For information, write to Special Sales Department, Newmarket Press, 18 East 48th Street, New York, NY 10017; call (212) 832-3575 or 1-800-669-3903; fax (212) 832-3629; or email info@newmarketpress.com.

www.newmarketpress.com

Manufactured in the United States of America

CONTENTS

Egyptian President Anwar el-Sadat (left) *and Israeli Prime Minister Menachem Begin* (right) *with President Jimmy Carter at the White House (1978).*

FOREWORD

BY PRESIDENT JIMMY CARTER
The Carter Presidential Library

"In our private and individual lives, all of us have a need to seek for heroes. In our own personal ambitions and life—analysis of what opportunities present themselves to us, the talents that we have, the unpredictable future—we need those on whom we can depend as a pattern. How can we live an exemplary existence? The measurement of that, the pattern for it, the guide for our own lives, comes from our heroes. How can we justify our dreams? How can we confirm our beliefs? How can we prove to ourselves that what we have been taught as children is true? How can we alleviate our doubts? How can we, in our own often naturally dormant lives, be inspired to action, sometimes even at the sacrifice of our own immediate well-being? We derive those inspirations from heroes."

These are my considered thoughts about heroes, presented in a speech in 1986. The Nobel Peace Prize was established to honor the heroes of peace, and this small book presents a collection of well-chosen excerpts from their addresses at Oslo, drawn both from acceptance speeches and from the lectures which each prize winner is expected to deliver.

The heroes of peace whose words are to be found here have followed a variety of paths toward their goal. Alfred Nobel had specified in his will that his prize was to be given for the organizing of peace congresses and efforts for disarmament, but also for work for "fraternity between nations." Beginning with the very first prize in 1901, the Norwegian Nobel

Committee has used the last phrase to interpret peacemaking ever more broadly.

While the majority of the early prizes went to peace activists, such as Nobel's friend Baroness Bertha von Suttner, prizes have been given away to many statesmen. The first of these went to President Theodore Roosevelt in 1906 for his role in negotiating an end to the Russo-Japanese War. Most recently, President Oscar Arias Sánchez won the prize in 1987 for his Central American Peace Plan, which has since contributed so much to bringing peace to that troubled area. I am especially happy to find represented in this volume my collaborators in the peacemaking of Camp David, Menachem Begin and Anwar Sadat, who was to die so tragically as a martyr to those efforts.

Heroes of peace to be found in these pages represent a great diversity: leaders of Red Cross organizations, whose work in the midst of violence has testified to the existence of the bonds of humanity; great humanitarians like Fridtjof Nansen and his successors in the Office of the United Nations High Commissioner for Refugees, who have sought to care for the millions who have been uprooted from their homeland in this war-torn century; others, such as Albert Schweitzer and Mother Teresa, whose acts of charity were inspired by their deep religious faith; religious leaders like Archbishop Söderblom and the Dalai Lama of Tibet, who emphasized that peace must first come to the human heart; scientists like Lord Boyd-Orr and Norman Borlaug, who worked for peace by bringing more food to a hungry world; other scientists like Linus Pauling, Evgeny Chazov, and Bernard Lown, who tried to prevent the nuclear catastrophe that their science told them might end life on this planet; apostles of disarmament like Philip Noel-Baker and Alva Myrdal; practitioners of nonviolence, such as the Quakers and the Peace People of Northern Ireland; and United Nations peacemakers, such as Ralph Bunche and Pérez de Cuéllar.

I have been happy to see the prize given more frequently in recent years to champions of human rights, who have a special section in this book. They include opponents of apartheid in South Africa, Chief Albert Lutuli and Archbishop Desmond Tutu; Martin Luther King, Jr., who fought and died for civil rights for all North Americans; Pérez Esquivel, who was imprisoned and tortured for his peace witness in Argentina; Andrei Sakharov, who lived just long enough to see his sacrifices for human rights begin to bear fruit in the Soviet Union; Lech Wałesa, who led the struggle for workers' rights in Poland; Elie Wiesel, who will not let the world forget the atrocities wreaked on human beings in the Holocaust; and the leaders of Amnesty International, who defend the rights of prisoners of conscience throughout the world.

I am convinced that for peace to endure, it must encompass justice, and I am confident that we can perceive today an inexorable trend toward the enhancement of human rights.

We need many kinds of peacemakers. We need those who work to resolve civil wars and international conflicts. We also need those who can establish ways to control and to reduce armaments. Preventing nuclear holocaust remains the highest priority.

We must also work to establish social and political conditions in which all human beings can enjoy freedom and the fullest measure of happiness. I think of those who struggle nonviolently for human rights, those who fight disease and poverty and hunger, and those who work to improve and preserve our environment. But even these efforts to build sound foundations for peace are in themselves not enough. Nobel's "fraternity between nations," the spirit of human brother-hood, must undergird any political or social structure of peace if it is to last. Archbishop Söderblom refers to this in these pages as the "soul" of such a structure; Albert Schweitzer speaks of it here as "the ethical spirit."

I have seen this spirit at work in men and women of myriad religious faiths and philosophical beliefs. I have found it in the volunteers of Habitat for Humanity, with whom Rosalynn and I have erected homes for the homeless. I have found it in the heroes I have come to know as the recipients of the human rights prize which Mrs. Dominique de Menil and I have established. And I have found it in world leaders like my martyred friend President Sadat.

Many of the heroes of peace who speak to us in these pages have spoken far more vibrantly in their deeds, motivated by this spirit. As we have found inspiration in their work for peace, so may we find inspiration in this excellent collection of their "Words of Peace."

INTRODUCTION

BY PROFESSOR JAKOB SVERDRUP
Former Director
The Norwegian Nobel Institute
Oslo, Norway

In 1901 the first Peace Prize was awarded. The years that have followed that award have not been very peaceful. It can be said that the twentieth century has been one of the most warlike centuries in Western history. Alfred Nobel would certainly have been disappointed if he had lived to see what came to happen in Europe: two bloody world wars and armament build-ups with incredibly destructive weapons. Have all his hopes for a peaceful world proved to be an illusion? I think it is more correct to say that Alfred Nobel was ahead of his time. If he had lived today, he would have been even more engaged in work for peace. And he would have seen that the idea of peace has much stronger support today than ninety-five years ago—in spite of, or rather because of, what has happened since he wrote his last will.

Peace is first of all the absence of war between states. That means that an international state dominated by power politics has to be replaced by an international system that makes it possible to resolve conflicts by means other than the use of arms. It has been a central task for peace workers to establish a system based on international law and peaceful solutions to conflicts—an aim strongly supported by two great American presidents, Woodrow Wilson and Franklin D. Roosevelt.

The Peace Prizes that have been awarded tell us, however, that peace means more than just the absence of war. Peace is also the absence of suppression and injustice. When people live with suppression, hunger, and lack of any hope for the future, conflicts will arise and the chance of war increases. Only international solidarity with people living under unjust conditions can create a more peaceful world.

In later years the Norwegian Nobel Committee, through its awards, has stressed the importance of human rights and justice. Equality between different races has been stressed through awards to Albert Lutuli, Martin Luther King, Jr., and Desmond Tutu. The prizes to Andrei Sakharov and Lech Wałesa mark a protest against the suppression of human rights in authoritarian societies. It has been encouraging to see that what has occurred in the last years in the field of human rights has been in the direction that these awards have tried to stimulate.

There will almost always be controversy connected with the award of the Peace Prizes. There is a wide spectrum of very different ideas on the question of what measures will best serve the cause of peace. And when the Prize is awarded to a fighter for human rights, the Nobel Committee is often accused of interfering in the domestic affairs of other states. It is an international concern in the same way as the struggle against poverty and the threat against our environment are concerns for the whole international community. We are rapidly moving in a direction where we have to find international solutions to the problems we are facing.

The Nobel prize winners have an obligation to deliver the Nobel lecture. Formerly this was usually presented the day after the Peace Prize ceremony. While at the ceremony the winner made a short speech of thanks. Now the winner expresses thanks and gives the lecture as part of the ceremony. At these times the winner has had an opportunity to present ideas on what he or she thinks are the most important peace issues we are facing. Their thoughts are well documented in the selections Professor Irwin Abrams has carefully chosen for this book.

The struggle for peace goes on continuously. Willy Brandt tells us something very important in a few sentences: "Peace, like freedom, is no original state which existed from the start; we shall have to make it, in the truest sense of the word."

Ralph Bunche, Undersecretary of the United Nations, with his family as he leaves from New York for the Congo to oversee UN operations there (1963).

PEACE

"The stars of eternal truth and right have always shone in the firmament of human understanding. The process of bringing them down to earth, remolding them into practical forms, imbuing them with vitality, and then making use of them has been a long one.

"One of the eternal truths is that happiness is created and developed in peace, and one of the eternal rights is the individual's right to live. The strongest of all instincts, that of self-preservation, is an assertion of this right, affirmed and sanctified by the ancient commandment: Thou shalt not kill."

—*BERTHA VON SUTTNER* (1905)*

"The adherents of the old order have a powerful ally in the natural law of inertia inherent in humanity which is, as it were, a natural defense against change. Thus pacifism faces no easy struggle. This question of whether violence or law shall prevail between states is the most vital of the problems of our eventful era, and the most serious in its repercussions. The beneficial results of a secure world peace are almost inconceivable, but even more inconceivable are the consequences of the threatening world war which many misguided people are prepared to precipitate. The advocates of pacifism are well aware how meager are their resources of personal influence and power. They know that they are still few in number and weak in authority, but when they realistically consider themselves and the ideal they serve, they see themselves as the servants of the greatest of all causes."

—*BERTHA VON SUTTNER* (1905)

The italicized date at the end of each selection and in the biographical entries represents the year for which the prize was awarded; on several occasions the Nobel Committee postponed its decision for a certain year and then made the grant of that year's prize one year later.

"Man's greatest advances these last few generations have been made by the application of human intelligence to the management of matter. Now we are confronted by a more difficult problem, the application of intelligence to the management of human relations. Unless we can advance in that field also, the very instruments that man's intelligence has created may be the instruments of his destruction.

"The obstacles to peace are not obstacles in matter, in inanimate nature, in the mountains which we pierce, in the seas across which we fly. The obstacles to peace are in the minds and hearts of men.

"In the study of matter we can be honest, impartial, true. That is why we succeed in dealing with it. But about the things we care for—which are ourselves, our desires and lusts, our patriotisms and hates—we find a harder test of thinking straight and truly. Yet there is the greater need. Only by intellectual rectitude and in that field shall we be saved. There is no refuge but in truth, in human intelligence, in the unconquerable mind of man."

—NORMAN ANGELL   (1933)

"Not long before the war the familiar doctrine was stated by a British cabinet minister at a great meeting in Manchester in some such terms as these: 'There is just one way in which we may have peace and be secure; and that is to be so much stronger than any potential enemy that he will not dare attack us. This I submit is a self-evident proposition.'

"Whereupon a thousand or so hardheaded businessmen of Manchester cheered to the echo. The proposition they were cheering was that two nations likely to quarrel would keep the peace and be secure when each was stronger than the other. It is possible that most, on second thoughts, would be brought to see that the principle does indeed defy arithmetic, but the vast majority would be sincerely astonished if it were suggested that this method of defense also defies morals, is based upon a flat denial of right, in the sense that each denies to the other the right he claims for himself.

"By that policy a nation, in order to be secure in its defense, has to be stronger than its potential enemy. Then what becomes of the defense of that other? Is he to have none?"

—*NORMAN ANGELL (1933)*

"A dark and terrible side of this sense of community of interests is the fear of a horrible common destiny which in these days of atomic weapons darkens men's minds all around the globe. Men have a sense of being subject to the same fate, of being all in the same boat. But fear is a poor motive to which to appeal, and I am sure that 'peace people' are on a wrong path when they expatiate on the horrors of a new world war. Fear weakens the nerves and distorts the judgment. It is not by fear that mankind must exorcise the demon of destruction and cruelty, but by motives more reasonable, more humane, and more heroic."

—*EMILY GREENE BALCH (1946)*

"If the target of output were the satisfaction of human needs, there would be no difficulty about markets. When the United States was battling with unemployment, the late President Roosevelt said that there were so many people ill-fed, ill-clothed, and ill-housed that if their needs were to be satisfied, there would be work for every man and woman willing to work. If that were true of the United States, how much truer is it of the world in which two out of every three people suffer premature death for the lack of the primary necessities of life. The upsurge in Asia, which is liable to spread to all colored races, is fundamentally a revolt against hunger and poverty. There can be no peace in the world so long as a large proportion of the population lacks the necessities of life and believes that a change of the political and economic system will make them available. World peace must be based on world plenty."

—*JOHN BOYD-ORR* (1949)

"Peace is no mere matter of men fighting or not fighting. Peace, to have meaning for many who have known only suffering in both peace and war, must be translated into bread or rice, shelter, health, and education, as well as freedom and human dignity—a steadily better life. If peace is to be secure, long-suffering and long-starved, forgotten peoples of the world, the underprivileged and the undernourished, must begin to realize without delay the promise of a new day and a new life."

—*RALPH J. BUNCHE* (1950)

"There will be no security in our world, no release from agonizing tension, no genuine progress, no enduring peace, until, in Shelley's fine words, 'reason's voice, loud as the voice of nature, shall have waked the nations.'"

—*RALPH J. BUNCHE* (1950)

"Defeatism about the future is a crime. The danger is not in trying to do too much, but in trying to do too little. [Fridtjof]

Nansen said here in 1926 that 'in the big things of life, it is vitally important to leave no line of retreat. . . . We must destroy the bridges behind us which lead back to the old policy and the old system, both of which are such utter failures.'

"In the age when the atom has been split, the moon encircled, diseases conquered, is disarmament so difficult a matter that it must remain a distant dream? To answer 'Yes' is to despair of the future of mankind."

—*PHILIP NOEL-BAKER*   *(1959)*

"All that I have said boils down to the point of affirming that mankind's survival is dependent upon man's ability to solve the problems of racial injustice, poverty, and war; the solution of these problems is in turn dependent upon man's squaring his moral progress with his scientific progress, and learning the practical art of living in harmony."

—*MARTIN LUTHER KING, JR.*   *(1964)*

"The destiny of world civilization depends upon providing a decent standard of living for all mankind. The guiding principles of the recipient of the 1969 Nobel Peace Price, the International Labor Organization, are expressed in its charter words, 'Universal and lasting peace can be established only if it is based upon social justice. If you desire peace, cultivate justice.' This is magnificent; no one can disagree with this lofty principle.

"Almost certainly, however, the first essential component of social justice is adequate food for all mankind. Food is the moral right of all who are born into this world. Yet today fifty percent of the world's population goes hungry. Without food, man can live at most but a few weeks; without it, all other components of social justice are meaningless. Therefore I feel that the aforementioned guiding principle must be modified to read: If you desire peace, cultivate justice, but at the same time cultivate the fields to produce more bread; otherwise there will be no peace."

—*NORMAN BORLAUG* *(1970)*

"Peace, like freedom, is no original state which existed from the start; we shall have to make it, in the truest sense of the word."

—*WILLY BRANDT* *(1971)*

"Peace is something more than the absence of war, although some nations would be thankful for that alone today. A durable and equitable peace system requires equal development opportunities for all nations."

—*WILLY BRANDT* *(1971)*

"If the attainment of peace is the ultimate objective of all statesmen, it is, at the same time, something very ordinary, closely tied to the daily life of each individual. In familiar terms, it is the condition that allows each individual and his family to pursue, without fear, the purpose of their lives. It is only in such circumstances that each individual will be able to devote himself, without the loss of hope for the future of mankind, to the education of his children, to an attempt to leave upon the history of mankind the imprint of his own creative and constructive achievements in the arts, culture, religion, and other activities fulfilling social aspirations. This is the peace which is essential for all individuals, peoples, nations, and thus for the whole of humanity."

—*EISAKU SATO* *(1974)*

"To the whole world, we repeat the same message that we proclaimed in August 1976. It is the Declaration of the Peace People:

'We have a simple message for the world from this movement for peace.

'We want to live and love and build a just and peaceful society.

'We want for our children, as we want for ourselves, lives at home, at work and at play to be lives of joy and peace.

'We recognize that to build such a life demands of all of us dedication, hard work and courage.

'We recognize that there are many problems in our society which are a source of conflict and violence.

'We recognize that every bullet fired and every exploding bomb makes that work more difficult.

'We reject the use of the bomb and the bullet and all the techniques of violence.

'We dedicate ourselves to working with our neighbors, near and far, day in and day out, to building that peaceful society in which the tragedies we have known are a bad memory and a continuing warning.'"

—*BETTY WILLIAMS* *(1976)*

"Peace is the beauty of life. It is sunshine. It is the smile of a child, the love of a mother, the joy of a father, the togetherness of a family. It is the advancement of man, the victory of a just cause, the triumph of truth. Peace is all of these and more and more.

"But in my generation, Ladies and Gentlemen, there was a time indescribable. Six million Jews—men, women and children—a number larger than many a nation in Europe—were dragged to a wanton death and slaughtered methodically in the heart of the civilized continent. . . . Those who were doomed, deprived of their human dignity, starved, humiliated, led away and ultimately turned into ashes cried out for rescue—but in vain.

"At such a time, unheard of since the first generation, the hour struck to rise and fight—for the dignity of man, for survival, for liberty, for every value of the human image a man has been endowed with by his Creator, for every known inalienable right he stands for and lives for. Indeed, there are days when to fight for a cause so absolutely just is the hardest human command. Norway has known such days, and so have we. Only in honoring that command comes the regeneration of the concept of peace. You rise, you struggle, you make sacrifices to achieve and guarantee the prospect of hope of living in peace—for you and your people, for your children and their children.

"Let it, however, be declared and known, stressed, and noted that fighters for freedom hate war. . . . This is our common maxim and belief—that if through your efforts and sacrifices you win liberty and with it the prospect of peace, then work for peace because there is no mission in life more sacred."

—*MENACHEM BEGIN* *(1978)*

"I repeat what I said in the Knesset more than a year ago:

'Any life lost in war is the life of a human being, irrespective of whether it is an Arab or an Israeli.

'The wife who becomes widowed is a human being, entitled to live in a happy family, Arab or Israeli.

'Innocent children, deprived of paternal care and sympathy, are all our children, whether they live on Arab or Israeli soil, and we owe them the biggest responsibility of providing them with a happy present and bright future.

'For the sake of all this, for the sake of protecting the lives of all our sons and brothers:

'For our societies to produce in security and confidence:

'For the development of man, his well-being and his right to share in an honorable life:

'For our responsibility toward the coming generations:

'For the smile of every child born on our land.'"

—*MOHAMMED ANWAR EL-SADAT* *(1978)*

" 'Peace is more than just absence of war. It is rather a state in which no people of any country, in fact no group of people of any kind live in fear or in need. . . .' Today, more than ten million refugees live in fear or in need. On our road towards a better future for mankind we certainly cannot ignore the tragic presence of those millions for whom peace does not exist. Whenever we solve one single problem we have contributed to peace for the individual. Whenever we bring peace to the individual we are making our world a slightly better place in which to live."

—*POUL HARTLING*, representing the Office of the
United Nations High Commissioner for refugees,
and quoting from the 1954 speech of
Dr. G. Jan van Heuven Goedhart *(1981)*

"Peace is not a matter of prizes or trophies. It is not the product of a victory or command. It has no finishing line, no final deadline, no fixed definition of achievement.

"Peace is a never-ending process, the work of many decisions by many people in many countries. It is an attitude, a way of life, a way of solving problems and resolving conflicts. It cannot be forced on the smallest nation or enforced by the largest. It cannot ignore our differences or overlook our common interests. It requires us to work and live together."

—OSCAR ARIAS SÁNCHEZ   (1987)

"Peace consists, very largely, in the fact of desiring it with all one's soul. The inhabitants of my small country, Costa Rica, have realized those words by Erasmus. Mine is an unarmed people, whose children have never seen a fighter or a tank or a warship."

—OSCAR ARIAS SÁNCHEZ   (1987)

"My country is a country of teachers. It is therefore a country of peace. We discuss our successes and failures in complete freedom. Because our country is a country of teachers, we closed the army camps, and our children go about with books under their arms, not with rifles on their shoulders. We believe in dialogue, in agreement, in reaching a consensus."

—OSCAR ARIAS SÁNCHEZ   (1987)

"Peace—the word evokes the simplest and most cherished dream of humanity. Peace is, and has always been, the ultimate human aspiration. And yet our history overwhelmingly shows that while we speak incessantly of peace, our actions tell a very different story.

"Peace is an easy word to say in any language. As Secretary-General of the United Nations, I hear it so frequently, from so many different mouths and different sources, that it sometimes seems to me to be a general incantation more or less deprived of practical meaning. What do we really mean by peace?

"Human nature being what it is, peace must inevitably be a relative condition. The essence of life is struggle and competition, and to that extent perfect peace is an almost meaningless abstraction. Struggle and competition are stimulating, but when they degenerate into conflict it is usually both destructive and disruptive. The aim of political institutions like the United Nations is to draw the line between struggle and conflict and to make it possible for nations to stay on the right side of that line. . . .

"These [peace-keeping forces] are soldiers without enemies. Their duty is to remain above the conflict. They may only use their weapons in the last resort for self-defense. Their strength is that, representing the will of the international community, they provide an honorable alternative to war and a useful pretext for peace. Their presence is often the essential prerequisite for negotiating a settlement. They have, or should have, a direct connection with the process of peacemaking."

—*JAVIER PÉREZ DE CUÉLLAR,* representing
the United Nations Peace-Keeping Forces
(1988)

"Peace, in the sense of the absence of war, is of little value to someone who is dying of hunger or cold. It will not remove the pain of torture inflicted on a prisoner of conscience. It does not comfort those who have lost their loved ones in floods caused by senseless deforestation in a neighboring country. Peace can only last where human rights are respected, where the people are fed, and where individuals and nations are free."

—*THE DALAI LAMA* *(1989)*

"Peace starts within each one of us. When we have inner peace, we can be at peace with those around us. When our community is in a state of peace, it can share that peace with neighboring communities, and so on. When we feel love and kindness towards others, it not only makes others feel loved and cared for, but it helps us also to develop inner happiness and peace."

—*THE DALAI LAMA* *(1989)*

"Today, peace means the ascent from simple coexistence to cooperation and common creativity among countries and nations.

"Peace is movement towards globality and universality of civilization. Never before has the idea that peace is indivisible been so true as it is now.

"Peace is not unity in similarity but unity in diversity, in the comparison and conciliation of differences.

"And, ideally, peace means the absence of violence. It is an ethical value."

—*MIKHAIL GORBACHEV* *(1990)*

"Peace does not fare well where poverty and deprivation reign.

"It does not flourish where there is ignorance and a lack of education and information.

"Repression, injustice and exploitation are inimical with peace.

"Peace is gravely threatened by inter-group fear and envy and by the unleashing of unrealistic expectations.

"Racial, class and religious intolerance and prejudice are its mortal enemies."

—*FREDERIK W. DE KLERK*   *(1993)*

"Peace for us is an *asset and in our interest.* It is an absolute human asset that allows an individual to freely develop his individuality unbound by any regional, religious or ethnic fetters. It restores to Arab–Israeli relations their innocent nature, and enables the Arab spirit to reflect through unrestrained human expression its profound understanding of the Jewish-European tragedy, just as it allows the tortured Jewish spirit to express its unfettered empathy for the suffering endured by the Palestinian people over their ruptured history. Only the tortured can understand those who have endured torture."

—*YASIR ARAFAT*   *(1994)*

"The most intractable of security problems is likely to be the one that relates not to the tools of conflict—to weapons and military forces—but to the roots of conflict in the inadequacies of the economic and environmental circumstances of a majority of the world's people. The overwhelming economic and environmental predicaments of the poor cannot be solved by the poor alone without substantial cooperation from the rich, and, conversely, the predicament of the poor cannot be allowed to persist without peril to the rich. We live under one atmosphere, on the shores of one ocean, our countries linked by flows of people, money, goods, weapons, drugs, diseases, and ideas. Either we will achieve an environmentally sustainable prosperity for all, in a world where weapons of mass destruction have disappeared or become irrelevant, or we will all suffer from the chaos, conflict, and destruction resulting from the failure to achieve this."

—*JOHN P. HOLDREN,* representing the
Pugwash Conferences on Science and World
Affairs *(1995)*

"Let it be stated clearly that to make peace a reality, we must be flexible as well as wise. We must truly recognize our own faults and move to change ourselves in the interest of making peace. I am no exception to this rule! Let us banish anger and hostility, vengeance and other dark emotions, and transform ourselves into humble instruments of peace. People in East Timor are not uncompromising. They are not unwilling to forgive and overcome their bitterness. On the contrary, they yearn for peace, peace within their community and peace in their region. They wish to build bridges with their Indonesian brothers and sisters, to find ways of creating harmony and tolerance."

—*CARLOS FILIPE XIMENES BELO* *(1996)*

"In my own work for peace, I was very strongly inspired by my European experience. I always tell this story, and I do so because it is so simple yet so profound and so applicable to conflict resolution anywhere in the world. On my first visit to

Strasbourg in 1979 as a member of the European Parliament, I went for a walk across the bridge from Strasbourg to Kehl. Strasbourg is in France. Kehl is in Germany. They are very close. I stopped in the middle of the bridge and I meditated. There is Germany. There is France. If I had stood on this bridge thirty years ago after the end of the Second World War when twenty-five million people lay dead across our continent for the second time in this century and if I had said: 'Don't worry. In thirty years' time we will all be together in a new Europe, our conflicts and wars will be ended and we will be working together in our common interests,' I would have been sent to a psychiatrist. But it has happened and it is now clear that European Union is the best example in the history of the world of conflict resolution and it is the duty of everyone, particularly those who live in areas of conflict to study how it was done and to apply its principles to their own conflict resolution."

—*JOHN HUME* *(1998)*

"I want to see Ireland as an example to men and women everywhere of what can be achieved by living for ideals, rather than fighting for them, and by viewing each and every person as worthy of respect and honour. I want to see an Ireland of partnership where we wage war on want and poverty, where we reach out to the marginalised and dispossessed, where we build together a future that can be as great as our dreams allow."

—*JOHN HUME* *(1998)*

"All conflict is about difference; whether the difference is race, religion, or nationality the European visionaries decided that difference is not a threat, difference is natural. Difference is of the essence of humanity. Difference is an accident of birth and it should therefore never be the source of hatred or conflict. The answer to difference is to respect it. Therein lies a most fundamental principle of peace: respect for diversity."

—*JOHN HUME* *(1998)*

"In this new century, we must start from the understanding that peace belongs not only to states or peoples, but to each and every member of those communities. The sovereignty of states must no longer be used as a shield for gross violations of human rights. Peace must be made real and tangible in the daily existence of every individual in need. Peace must be sought, above all, because it is the condition for every member of the human family to live a life of dignity and security.

"The rights of the individual are of no less importance to immigrants and minorities in Europe and the Americas than to women in Afghanistan or children in Africa. They are as fundamental to the poor as to the rich; they are as necessary to the security of the developed world as to that of the developing world."

—*KOFI ANNAN* *(2001)*

"In a world filled with weapons of war and all too often words of war, the Nobel Committee has become a vital agent for peace. Sadly, a prize for peace is a rarity in this world. Most nations have monuments or memorials to war, bronze salutations to heroic battles, archways of triumph. But peace has no parade, no pantheon of victory."

—*KOFI ANNAN* *(2001)*

"Instead of entering a millennium of peace, the world is now, in many ways, a more dangerous place. The greater ease of travel and communication has not been matched by equal understanding and mutual respect. There is a plethora of civil wars, unrestrained by rules of the Geneva Convention, within which an overwhelming portion of the casualties are unarmed civilians who have no ability to defend themselves. And recent appalling acts of terrorism have reminded us that no nations, even superpowers, are invulnerable.

"It is clear that global challenges must be met with an emphasis on peace, in harmony with others, with strong alliances and international consensus. Imperfect as it may be, there is no doubt that this can best be done through the United Nations, which Ralph Bunche described here in this same forum as exhibiting a 'fortunate flexibility'—not merely to preserve peace but also to make change, even radical change, without violence."

—*JIMMY CARTER (2002)*

"Although this prize comes to me, it acknowledges the work of countless individuals and groups across the globe. They work quietly and often without recognition to protect the environment, promote democracy, defend human rights, and ensure equality between women and men. By so doing, they plant seeds of peace. I know they, too, are proud today. To all who feel represented by this prize I say use it to advance your mission and meet the high expectations the world will place on us."

—*WANGARI MAATHAI (2004)*

"In the course of history, there comes a time when humanity is called to shift to a new level of consciousness, to reach a higher moral ground. A time when we have to shed our fear and give hope to each other.

"That time is now.

"The Norwegian Nobel Committee has challenged the world to broaden the understanding of peace: there can be no peace without equitable development; and there can be no development without sustainable management of the environment in a democratic and peaceful space. This shift is an idea whose time has come."

—WANGARI MAATHAI (2004)

"Poverty is a threat to peace.

"World's income distribution gives a very telling story. Ninety-four percent of the world income goes to 40 percent of the population, while 60 percent of people live on only 6 percent of world income. Half of the world population lives on two dollars a day. Over one billion people live on less than a dollar a day. This is no formula for peace."

—MUHAMMAD YUNUS (2006)

"Peace can be defined as security and the secure access to resources that are essential for living. A disruption in such access could prove disruptive of peace."

—R. K. PACHAURI, representing Intergovernmental Panel on Climate Change (2007)

Albert Schweitzer talking with a patient at his hospital near Lambarene, Gabon (1963).

THE
BONDS
OF
HUMANITY

"If a present-day prophet were to exhort the peoples to peace and common sense, he would speak as one human being to others. With the power of the law and the gentleness of the Gospel, he would speak thus: 'Patriotism is a noble feeling, insofar as it approaches that which is purely human, but the very reverse the further it is removed therefrom. No interests, however great, are higher than those common to the whole of mankind. Among them, the foremost is the old commandment, as old as the oldest documents of any nation: Thou shalt not kill! You are all of one blood. Love one another. People can. Nations can. All this is eminently possible because love is as natural as national hatred is the most unnatural of all human feelings.'"

—*KLAUS PONTUS ARNOLDSON* *(1908)*

"But more important by far than any political disarmament of armies and fleets is the 'disarmament' of the people from within, the generation, in fact, of sympathy in the souls of men."

—*FRIDTJOF NANSEN* *(1922)*

"The festival of Christmas is approaching, when the message to mankind is: Peace on earth.

"Never has suffering and bewildered mankind awaited the Prince of Peace with greater longing, the Prince of Charity who holds aloft a white banner bearing the one word inscribed in golden letters: 'Work.'

"All of us can become workers in his army on its triumphant march across the earth to raise a new spirit in a new generation—to bring men love of their fellowmen and an honest desire for peace—to bring back the will to work and the joy of work—to bring faith in the dawn of a new day."

—FRIDTJOF NANSEN (1922)

"To contrast national solidarity and international cooperation as two opposites seems foolish to me. As Germany's representative in Geneva, I expressed the belief that it cannot have been intended in the divine plan that man's noblest abilities should be working in opposition to one another. I tried to make the point that the man who cultivates to the highest degree the qualities inherent in his national culture will gain insight into universal knowledge and feeling which transcend the limitations of his own heritage; and he will create works which, like cathedrals, although built upon the soil of his native land, will soar into the heaven of all mankind. A Shakespeare could have arisen only on English soil. In the same way, your great dramatists and poets express the nature and essence of the Norwegian people, but they also express that which is universally valid for all mankind. . . . National culture can act as a bridge, instead of an obstacle, to mutual spiritual and intellectual understanding. The great men of a nation reach out to all mankind. They are unifying, not divisive; internationally conciliating and still great nationally."

—GUSTAV STRESEMANN (1926)

"The policy I have endeavored to sketch is big, bold, and far-reaching. It will be no light and simple task to lay the foundations of a World Commonwealth. It is, on the contrary, perhaps, the greatest and most difficult enterprise ever imagined by the audacious mind of man. But it is a task which has become a necessity. It is an enterprise that is solidly grounded in realities and in the facts of the modern world. If there is still virtue in our common Western civilization and our faith in democracy—and I believe there is—then we must dare to announce that policy as a challenge to the world and as the summons to a great crusade for peace. What greater cause and what more splendid adventure can be set before the youth of the world than the endeavor to bring into being that age-old dream of saints and sages—the great Commonwealth of the World as the visible embodiment of the brotherhood of man?"

—*ARTHUR HENDERSON* *(1934)*

"The common people of all nations want peace. In the presence of great impersonal forces they feel individually helpless to promote it. You are saying to them here today that common folk, not statesmen, nor generals, nor great men of affairs, but just simple plain men and women like the few thousand Quakers and their friends, if they devote themselves to resolute insistence on goodwill in place of force, even in the face of great disaster past or threatened, can do something to build a better, peaceful world. The future hope of peace lies with such personal sacrificial service. To this ideal humble persons everywhere may contribute."

—*HENRY J. CADBURY,* representing the American Friends Service Committee *(1947)*

"The spirit is not dead; it lives in isolation. It has overcome the difficulty of having to exist in a world out of harmony with its ethical character. It has come to realize that it can find no home other than in the basic nature of man. . . .

"It is convinced that compassion, in which ethics takes root, does not assume its true proportions until it embraces not only man but every living being. To the old ethics, which lacked this depth and force of conviction, has been added the ethics of reverence for life, and its validity is steadily gaining in recognition."

—*ALBERT SCHWEITZER* *(1952)*

"Their [the League of Nations' and the United Nations'] efforts were doomed to fail since they were obliged to undertake them in a world in which there was no prevailing spirit directed toward peace. And being only legal institutions, they were unable to create such a spirit. The ethical spirit alone has the power to generate it. Kant deceived himself in thinking that he could dispense with it in his search for peace. We must follow the road on which he turned his back."

—*ALBERT SCHWEITZER* *(1952)*

"Is the spirit capable of achieving what we in our distress must expect of it?

"Let us not underestimate its power, the evidence of which can be seen throughout the history of mankind. The spirit created this humanitarianism which is the origin of all progress toward some form of higher existence. Inspired by humanitarianism we are true to ourselves and capable of creating. Inspired by a contrary spirit we are unfaithful to ourselves and fall prey to all manner of error."

—*ALBERT SCHWEITZER* *(1952)*

"But Kant's reliance on the people's innate love for peace has not been justified. Because the will of the people, being the will of the crowd, has not avoided the danger of instability and the risk of emotional distraction from the path of true reason, it has failed to demonstrate a vital sense of responsibility. Nationalism of the worst sort was displayed in the last two wars, and it may be regarded today as the greatest obstacle to mutual understanding between peoples.

"Such nationalism can be repulsed only through the rebirth of a humanitarian ideal among men which will make their allegiance to their country a natural one inspired by genuine ideals. . . .

"All men, even the semicivilized and the primitive, are, as beings capable of compassion, able to develop a humanitarian spirit. It abides within them like tinder ready to be lit, waiting only for a spark."

—*ALBERT SCHWEITZER* (1952)

"I am well aware that what I have had to say on the problem of peace is not essentially new. It is my profound conviction that the solution lies in our rejecting war for an ethical reason; namely, that war makes us guilty of the crime of inhumanity. . . .

"The only originality I claim is that for me this truth goes hand in hand with the intellectual certainty that the human spirit is capable of creating in our time a new mentality, an ethical mentality. Inspired by this certainty, I too proclaim this truth in the hope that my testimony may help to prevent its rejection as an admirable sentiment but a practical impossibility. Many a truth has lain unnoticed for a long time, ignored simply because no one perceived its potential for becoming reality.

"Only when an ideal of peace is born in the minds of the peoples will the institutions set up to maintain this peace effectively fulfill the function expected of them."

—*ALBERT SCHWEITZER*   *(1952)*

"There can be no real peace in this world as long as hundreds of thousands of men, women and children, through no fault of their own, but only because they sacrificed all they possessed for the sake of what they believed, still remain in camps and live in misery and in the greatest uncertainty of their future. Eventually, if we wait too long, the uprooted are bound to become easy prey for political adventurers, from whom the world has suffered too much already. Before anything of that sort happens, let us join our hands in an all-out effort to solve their problem.

"Many years ago I participated in a discussion on the problem of international education. After many experts had presented their complicated theories, an old headmaster of a certain school got up and quietly said: 'There is only one system of education, through love and one's own example.' He was right. What is true for education is true also for the refugee problem of today. With love and our own example—example in the sense of sacrifice—it can be solved. And if in the cynical times in which we live someone might be inclined to laugh at 'love' and 'example' as factors in politics, he would do well to be reminded of Nansen's hard-hitting, direct, and courageous words, based on a life full of sacrifice and devotion: 'Love of man is practical policy.' "

—*DR. G. JAN VAN HEUVEN GOEDHART,*
representing the Office of United Nations
Commissioner for Refugees   *(1954)*

"That problem, why men fight who aren't necessarily fighting men, was posed for me in a new and dramatic way one Christmas Eve in London during World War II. The air-raid sirens had given their grim and accustomed warning. Almost before the last dismal moan had ended, the anti-aircraft guns began to crash. In between their bursts I could hear the deeper, more menacing sound of bombs. It wasn't much of a raid, really, but one or two of the bombs seemed to fall too close to my room. I was reading in bed and, to drown out or at least to take my mind off the bombs, I reached out and turned on the radio. I was fumbling aimlessly with the dial when the room was flooded with the beauty and peace of Christmas carol music. Glorious waves of it wiped out the sound of war and conjured up visions of happier peacetime Christmases. Then the announcer spoke—in German—for it was a German station and they were Germans who were singing those carols. Nazi bombs screaming through the air with their message of war and death; German music drifting through the air with its message of peace and salvation. When we resolve the paradox of those two sounds from a single national source, we will, at last, be in a good position to understand and solve the problem of peace and war."

—*LESTER B. PEARSON* *(1957)*

"Let us be wary of mass solutions, let us be wary of statistics. We must love our neighbors as ourselves. . . . There is perhaps no surer road to peace than the one that starts from little islands and oases of genuine kindness, islands and oases constantly growing in number and being continually joined together until eventually they ring the world."

—*FATHER DOMINIQUE PIRE* *(1958)*

"The sacred union existing between two brother human beings who rediscover themselves as men of true dignity while working together to save a third rids us of many of the barriers of prejudice, narrow-mindedness, and discrimination that poison human love and sap its strength. We must now have faith in the power of love and set it to work. Let me point out right away that a gesture of brotherly love extended jointly requires no compromise of principle, but on the contrary is justified and indeed welcomed by the right-minded. Let us not speak of *tolerance*. This negative word implies grudging concessions by smug consciences. Rather, let us speak of mutual understanding and mutual respect."

—*FATHER DOMINIQUE PIRE* (1958)

"In a strife-torn world, tottering on the brink of complete destruction by man-made nuclear weapons, a free and independent Africa is in the making, in answer to the injunction and challenge of history: 'Arise and shine for thy light is come.' Acting in concert with other nations, she is man's last hope for a mediator between the East and West, and is qualified to demand of the great powers to 'turn the swords into ploughshares' because two-thirds of mankind is hungry and illiterate; to engage human energy, human skill, and human talent in the service of peace, for the alternative is unthinkable—war, destruction, and desolation; and to build a world community which will stand as a lasting monument to the millions of men and women, to such devoted and distinguished world citizens and fighters for peace as the late Dag Hammarskjöld, who have given their lives that we may live in happiness and peace.

"Africa's qualification for this noble task is incontestable, for her own fight has never been and is not now a fight for conquest of land, for accumulation of wealth or domination of peoples, but for the recognition and preservation of the rights of man and the establishment of a truly free world for a free people."

—*ALBERT JOHN LUTULI* *(1960)*

"Is the Red Cross in wartime a flickering flame to remind us of our continuing brotherhood? Is it a gesture to declare, despite appearances, that we are derived from the Godhead; that we may lay waste our bodies but cannot cast aside, entirely, our souls?

"It is this contrast between the work of the Red Cross in peace and in war that provides an endless fascination. In peace, it is the strong support of beneficent service, and in emergencies a wave and pillar of succor for the distressed. In war, it is a liaison, a medium of practical help to the wounded and the prisoner, a symbol that beyond the knives and guns, the larks and the angels are watching."

—*JOHN A. MACAULAY,* representing the
League of Red Cross Societies *(1963)*

"A famous poet once inquired: 'Where are the snows of yesteryear?' Perhaps we shall live to the day when men will ask: 'Where are the hates of yesteryear?' For, in the long run, the power of kindness can redeem beyond the power of force to destroy. There is a vast reservoir of kindness that we can no longer afford to disregard.

"The curtain is lifting. We can have Triumph or Tragedy—for we are the playwrights, the actors, and the audience. Let us book our seats for Triumph—the world is sickened of Tragedy."

—*JOHN A. MACAULAY,* representing the
League of Red Cross Societies *(1963)*

"Today I come to Oslo as a trustee, inspired and with renewed dedication to humanity. I accept this prize on behalf of all men who love peace and brotherhood. I say I come as a trustee, for in the depths of my heart I am aware that this prize is much more than an honor to me personally.

"Every time I take a flight, I am always mindful of the many people who make a successful journey possible—the known pilots and the unknown ground crew. You honor the dedicated pilots of our struggle who have sat at the controls as the freedom movement soared into orbit. You honor, once again, Chief Lutuli of South Africa, whose struggles with and for his people, are still met with the most brutal expression of man's inhumanity to man. You honor the ground crew without whose labor and sacrifice the jet flights to freedom could never have left the earth. Most of these people will never make the headlines and their names will not appear in *Who's Who.* Yet when years have rolled past and when the blazing light of truth is focused on this marvelous age in which we live—men and women will know and children will be taught that we have a finer land, a better people, a more noble civilization—because these humble children of god were willing to suffer for righteousness' sake.

"I think Alfred Nobel would know what I mean when I say that I accept this award in the spirit of a curator of some precious heirloom which he holds in trust for its true owners—all those to whom beauty is truth and truth beauty—and in

31

whose eyes the beauty of genuine brotherhood and peace is more precious than diamonds or silver or gold."

—*MARTIN LUTHER KING, JR.*   *(1964)*

"The voice of women has a special role and a special soulforce in the struggle for a nonviolent world. We do not wish to replace religious sectarianism or ideological division with sexism or any kind of militant feminism. But we do believe that women have a leading role to play in this great struggle.

"So we are honored, in the name of all women, that women have been honored especially for their part in leading a nonviolent movement for a just and peaceful society. Compassion is more important than intellect in calling forth the love that the work of peace needs, and intuition can often be a far more powerful searchlight than cold reason. We have to think, and think hard, but if we do not have compassion before we even start thinking, then we are quite likely to start fighting over theories. . . .

"Because of the role of women over so many centuries in so many different cultures, they have been excluded from what have been called public affairs; for that very reason they have concentrated much more on things close to home . . . and they have kept far more in touch with the true realities . . . the realities of giving birth and love. The moment has perhaps come in human history when, for very surival, those realities must be given pride of place over the vainglorious adventures that lead to war.

"But we do not wish to see a division over this . . . merely a natural and respectful and loving cooperation. Women and men together can make this a beautiful people's world, and that is why we called ourselves 'THE PEACE PEOPLE.'"

—*BETTY WILLIAMS* *(1976)*

"At times our members have gained more from the prisoner they sought to help than the prisoner has gained from them: much of courage, of the value of human dignity and freedom, of the durability of the human spirit.

"It is for this reason that our last word should belong to a prisoner.

"Some time ago, one of them, now dead, was able to send a letter from prison in which she wrote:

"They are envious of us. They will envy us all, for it is an enviable but very difficult task to live through a history as a human being, to complete a life as a human being. Soon the night will fall and they will close the doors of the cell. I feel lonely. No . . . I am with the whole of mankind and the whole of mankind is with me."

—*MÜMTAZ SOYSAL,* representing Amnesty International *(1977)*

"From this platform of peace, I would like to appeal to all those in whose hands the future of mankind lies, to use their power not to destroy or kill, not to create suffering in a grasping search for selfish objectives, but to help alleviate the plight of the needy; to aim at justice and freedom for the individual.

"And I appeal to each and every one. Let us never cease to feel compassion for those in want. Let us never tire of helping victims of injustice and oppression. He who puts his faith in the restoration of human dignity cannot be wrong."

—*POUL HARTLING,* representing the Office of the United Nations High Commissioner for Refugees *(1981)*

"I come from a beautiful land, richly endowed by God with wonderful natural resources, wide expanses, rolling mountains, singing birds, bright shining stars out of blue skies, with radiant sunshine, golden sunshine. There is enough of the good things that come from God's bounty, there is enough for everyone, but apartheid has confirmed some in their selfishness, causing them to grasp greedily a disproportionate share, the lion's share, because of their power."

—*DESMOND MPILO TUTU (1984)*

"There is no peace in Southern Africa. There is no peace because there is no justice. There can be no real peace and security until there be first justice enjoyed by all the inhabitants of that beautiful land. The Bible knows nothing about peace without justice, for that would be crying, 'Peace, peace, where there is no peace.' God's Shalom, peace, involves inevitably righteousness, justice, wholeness, fullness of life, participation in decision making, goodness, laughter, joy, compassion, sharing, and reconciliation."

—*DESMOND MPILO TUTU (1984)*

"Because there is global insecurity, nations are engaged in a mad arms race, spending billions of dollars wastefully on instruments of destruction, when millions are starving. And yet, just a fraction of what is expended so obscenely on defense budgets would make the difference in enabling God's children to fill their stomachs, be educated, and be given the chance to lead fulfilled and happy lives. We have the capacity to feed ourselves several times over, but we are daily haunted by the spectacle of the gaunt dregs of humanity shuffling along in endless queues, with bowls to collect what the charity of the world has provided, too little too late. When will we learn, when will the people of the world get up and say, Enough is enough. God created us for fellowship. God created us so that we should form the human family, existing together because we were made for one another. We are not made for an exclusive self-sufficiency but for interdependence, and we break the law of our being at our peril."

—*DESMOND MPILO TUTU*   (1984)

"The problems we face today, violent conflicts, destruction of nature, poverty, hunger, and so on, are human-created problems which can be resolved through human effort, understanding and the development of a sense of brotherhood and sisterhood. We need to cultivate a universal responsibility for one another and the planet we share. Although I have found my own Buddhist religion helpful in generating love and compassion, even for those we consider our enemies, I am convinced that everyone can develop a good heart and a sense of universal responsibility with or without religion."

—*THE DALAI LAMA*   (1989)

"The value of our shared reward will and must be measured by the joyful peace which will triumph, because the common humanity that bonds both black and white into one human race, will have said to each one of us that we shall all live like the children of paradise.

"Thus shall we live, because we will have created a society which recognises that all people are born equal, with each entitled in equal measure to life, liberty, prosperity, human rights and good governance.

"Such a society should never allow again that there should be prisoners of conscience nor that any person's human rights should be violated."

—*NELSON MANDELA* (1993)

"Let it never be said by future generations that indifference, cynicism or selfishness made us fail to live up to the ideals of humanism which the Nobel Peace Prize encapsulates.

"Let the strivings of us all prove Martin Luther King, Jr., to have been correct, when he said that humanity can no longer be tragically bound to the starless midnight of racism and war.

"Let the efforts of us all prove that he was not a mere dreamer when he spoke of the beauty of genuine brotherhood and peace being more precious than diamonds or silver or gold.

"Let a new age dawn!"

—*NELSON MANDELA* (1993)

"Whatever system of governance is eventually adopted, it is important that it carries the people with it. We need to convey the message that safeguarding our common property, humankind, will require developing in each of us a new loyalty: a loyalty to mankind. It calls for the nurturing of a feeling of belonging to the human race. We have to become world citizens."

—*JOSEPH ROTBLAT* *(1995)*

"The fantastic advances in communication and transportation have shrunk our globe. All nations of the world have become close neighbours. Modern information techniques enable us to learn instantly about every event in every part of the globe. We can talk to each other via the various networks. This facility will improve enormously with time because the achievements so far have only scratched the surface. Technology is driving us together. In many ways we are becoming like one family. With the global threats resulting from science and technology, the whole of humankind now needs protection. We have to extend our loyalty to the whole of the human race."

—*JOSEPH ROTBLAT* *(1995)*

"Society is a succession of interwoven rings in which each generation has the duty to contribute to the next generation in order to live in the world peacefully, fraternally. Under your shoulders, dear young people of the entire world, weigh the responsibility to transform tomorrow's world into a society where peace, harmony, and fraternity reign."

—*CARLOS FILIPE XIMENES BELO* *(1996)*

"Anti-personnel mines do not only sever limbs, they can break the human spirit. We talk not of mine victims, but of survivors—but to survive trauma requires support, encouragement, and love. That responsibility must not be left to the survivors' family and friends, who are often struggling themselves against poverty and the damaging effects of conflict, but to a greater extent family—the human family."

—*RAE MCGRATH,* representing the
International Campaign to Ban Landmines
(1997)

"If conflicts and wars are an affair of the state, violations of humanitarian law, war crimes and crimes against humanity apply to us all—as civil society, as citizens, and as human beings."

—*JAMES ORBINSKI,* representing Médecins
Sans Frontières *(1999)*

"Humanitarian action is more than simple generosity, simple charity. It aims to build spaces of normalcy in the midst of what is profoundly abnormal. More than offering material assistance, we aim to enable individuals to regain their rights and dignity as human beings."

—*JAMES ORBINSKI,* representing Médecins
Sans Frontières *(1999)*

"For Médecins Sans Frontières, this is the humanitarian act: to seek to relieve suffering, to seek to restore autonomy, to witness to the truth of injustice, and to insist on political responsibility."

—*JAMES ORBINSKI,* representing Médecins
Sans Frontières *(1999)*

"We affirm the independence of the humanitarian from the political, but this is not to polarize the 'good' NGO against 'bad' governments, or the 'virtue' of civil society against the 'vice' of political power. Such a polemic is false and dangerous. As with slavery and welfare rights, history has shown that humanitarian pre-occupations born in civil society have gained influence until they reach the political agenda. But these convergences should not mask the distinctions that exist between the political and the humanitarian. Humanitarian action takes place in the short term, for limited groups and for limited objectives. This is at the same time both its strength and its limitation. The political can only be conceived in the long term, which itself is the movement of societies. Humanitarian action is by definition universal. Humanitarian responsibility has no frontiers. Wherever in the world there is manifest distress, the humanitarian by vocation, must respond."

—*JAMES ORBINSKI,* representing Médecins
Sans Frontières *(1999)*

"Despite grand debates on world order, the act of humanitarianism comes down to one thing: individual human beings reaching out to those others who find themselves in the most difficult circumstances. And they reach out one bandage at a time, one suture at a time, one vaccination at a time."

—*JAMES ORBINSKI,* representing Médecins
Sans Frontières *(1999)*

"We have entered the third millennium through a gate of fire. If today, after the horror of September 11, we see better, and we see further—we will realize that humanity is indivisible. New threats make no distinction between races, nations, or regions. A new insecurity has entered every mind, regardless of wealth or status. A deeper awareness of the bonds that bind us all—in pain as in prosperity—has gripped young and old."

—*KOFI ANNAN (2001)*

"Today, however, even amidst continuing ethnic conflict around the world, there is a growing understanding that human diversity is both the reality that makes dialogue necessary, and the very basis for that dialogue.

"We understand, as never before, that each of us is fully worthy of the respect and dignity essential to our common humanity. We recognize that we are the products of many cultures, traditions, and memories; that mutual respect allows us to study and learn from other cultures; and that we gain strength by combining the foreign with the familiar."

—*KOFI ANNAN (2001)*

"Each of us has the right to take pride in our particular faith or heritage. But the notion that what is ours is necessarily in conflict with what is theirs is both false and dangerous. It has resulted in endless enmity and conflict, leading men to commit the greatest of crimes in the name of a higher power.

"It need not be so. People of different religions and cultures live side by side in almost every part of the world, and most of us have overlapping identities which unite us with very different groups. We can love what we are, without hating what—and who—we are not. We can thrive in our own tradition, even as we learn from others, and come to respect their teachings."

—*Kofi Annan* *(2001)*

"War may sometimes be a necessary evil. But no matter how necessary, it is always an evil, never a good. We will not learn how to live together in peace by killing each other's children.

"The bond of our common humanity is stronger than the divisiveness of our fears and prejudices. God gives us the capacity for choice. We can choose to alleviate suffering. We can choose to work together for peace. We can make these changes—and we must."

—*Jimmy Carter* *(2002)*

"On the environment front, people are exposed to many human activities that are devastating to the environment and societies. These include widespread destruction of ecosystems, especially through deforestation, climatic instability, and contamination in the soils and waters that all contribute to excruciating poverty.

"In the process, the participants discover that they must be part of the solutions. They realize their hidden potential and are empowered to overcome inertia and take action. They come to recognize that they are the primary custodians and beneficiaries of the environment that sustains them.

"Entire communities also come to understand that while it is necessary to hold their governments accountable, it is equally important that in their own relationships with each other, they exemplify the leadership values they wish to see in their own leaders, namely justice, integrity, and trust."

—*WANGARI MAATHAI (2004)*

"Since the beginning of history, human beings have been at war with each other, under the pretext of religion, ideology, ethnicity and other reasons. And no civilization has ever willingly given up its most powerful weapons. We seem to agree today that we can share modern technology, but we still refuse to acknowledge that our values—at their very core—are shared values."

—*MOHAMED ELBARADEI (2005)*

"We now have the opportunity, more than at any time before, to give an affirmative answer to one of the oldest questions of all time: 'Am I my brother's keeper?'

"What is required is a new mindset and a change of heart, to be able to see the person across the ocean as our neighbor.

"Finally, I have hope because of what I see in my children, and some of their generation.

"I took my first trip abroad at the age of 19. My children were even more fortunate than I. They had their first exposure to foreign culture as infants, and they were raised in a multicultural environment. And I can say absolutely that my son and daughter are oblivious to color and race and nationality. They see no difference between their friends Noriko, Mafupo, Justin, Saulo, and Hussam; to them, they are only fellow human beings and good friends."

—*MOHAMED ELBARADEI (2005)*

"We, the human species, are confronting a planetary emergency—a threat to the survival of our civilization that is gathering ominous and destructive potential even as we gather here. But there is hopeful news as well: we have the ability to solve this crisis and avoid the worst—though not all—of its consequences, if we act boldly, decisively and quickly."

—*AL GORE, JR. (2007)*

"Neglect in protecting our heritage of natural resources could prove extremely harmful for the human race and for all species that share common space on planet earth. Indeed, there are many lessons in human history which provide adequate warning about the chaos and destruction that could take place if we remain guilty of myopic indifference to the progressive erosion and decline of nature's resources."

—*R. K. PACHAURI,* representing
Intergovernmental Panel on Climate
Change (2007)

Mother Teresa, founder of the Roman Catholic order Missionaries of Charity in Calcutta, hugging a child on a visit to New York (1981).

FAITH
AND
HOPE

"Consider the way that poets, with few exceptions, pay court to fame and popularity by singing the praises of war and massacre. Consider again how the most sublime virtues are always associated with the national flag while cruelty is ascribed to the enemy alone—this in order to sustain mistrust, hatred, and enmity between nations. Remembering and pondering all this, oh, I confess to you that I too have had moments of discouragement, wondering whether the idea to which I devote, and have for years devoted, all my time and energy might be no more than an illusion of my poor mind, a dream like Thomas More's *Utopia* or our own Campanella's *City of the Sun.*

"But these were fleeting moments! And I was soon telling myself that if work for a future of peace and justice, a future of continual progress and of fruitful and useful labor for all men and all nations, was indeed an illusion, it was still an illusion so divine as to make life worth living and to inspire one to die for it.

"But it is not an illusion. I felt this deep within me, and the history of human evolution as well as everyday experience confirmed it for me. Reasonable ideas which find their sanction in the conscience of the righteous do not die; they are consequently realities and active forces, but they are so only to the extent that those who profess them know how to turn them to account. It depends on us, then, and on our judgment and steadfastness whether or not the idea of peace will root itself ever more firmly in public awareness until it grows into the living and active conscience of a whole people."

—*ERNESTO TEODORO MONETA* *(1907)*

"To climb by all roads originating from all points of the world to the pinnacle where the law of man itself holds sway in sovereign rhythm—is this not the ultimate end of mankind's painful and centuries-long ascent of Calvary?

"To be sure, many years of trial must yet elapse, and many retrogressions yet occur, before the rumble of human passions common to all men yields to silence; but if the road toward the final goal is clearly marked, if an organization like the League of Nations realizes its potential and achieves its purpose, the potent benefits of peace and of human solidarity will triumph over evil. This at least we may dare to hope for; and, if we will consider how far we have come since the dawn of history, then our hope will gather strength enough to become a true and unshakable faith."

—*Léon Bourgeois* *(1920)*

"Therefore, all hope of a better future for mankind rests on the promotion of 'a higher form of development for world civilization,' an all-embracing human community. Are we right in adopting a teleological viewpoint, a belief that a radiant and beneficent purpose guides the fate of men and of nations and will lead us forward to that higher stage of social development? In propaganda work we must necessarily build upon such an optimistic assumption. Propaganda must appeal to mankind's better judgment and to the necessary belief in a better future. For this belief, the valley of the shadow of death is but a way station on the road to the blessed summit."

—*Christian L. Lange* *(1921)*

"There are surely many of us who can only regard the belief in personal immortality as a claim which must remain unproved— a projection of the eternity concept onto the personal level.

"Should we then be compelled to believe that the theory of materialism expressed in the old Arab parable of the bush whose leaves fall withered to the ground and die without leaving a trace behind truly applies to the family of man?

"It seems to me that the theory of mankind's organic unity and eternal continuity raises the materialistic view to a higher level.

"The idea of eternity lives in all of us. We thirst to live in a belief which raises our small personality to a higher coherence— a coherence which is human and yet superhuman, absolute and yet steadily growing and developing, ideal and yet real.

"Can this desire ever be fulfilled? It seems to be a contradiction in terms.

"And yet there is a belief which satisfies this desire and resolves the contradiction.

"It is the belief in the unity of mankind."

—*CHRISTIAN L. LANGE* *(1921)*

"If peace is to become a reality on our earth, it must be founded in the hearts of the people. To whom should this task belong if not to the church, which calls itself the Prince of Peace and has as its watchword what is also a divine promise: Glory to God in the highest and peace on earth. The human heart is fickle, and therefore peace must, according to the words of the prophets, be safeguarded by law and order, by a supranational judicial system which has the power to assert itself against nations endangering peace and which, without bias or compromise, holds justice to be the highest law. Nevertheless, any such legal system, however wise and strong, remains a mere shell if not supported by mankind's concern for peace and liberty. . . . But if a body does not possess a soul, it differs little from a machine. In this instance, the soul is the love and justice of the Gospel, not the demon of selfishness."

—*NATHAN SÖDERBLOM* *(1930)*

"We do not believe with Socrates that man does what is right because he knows it to be right, but we must agree with the philosopher in that man needs to know what is right before he acts."

—*NATHAN SÖDERBLOM* *(1930)*

"We must not stumble over the barriers we meet. We must run hard, for sometimes we must leap high to surmount the difficulties of fulfilling our obligations to humanity. We must not let ourselves be torn by the thorns of thickets obstructing the 'savage paths' of which I spoke earlier. We must look higher and at the same time nearer. We must draw close in body and in spirit in order to merit the name by which the magnificent symbol of the Red Cross calls us, the name Man, the name Christian."

—*ÉDOUARD CHAPUISAT,* representing the International Committee of the Red Cross *(1944)*

"I have spoken against fear as a basis for peace. What we ought to fear, especially we Americans, is not that someone may drop atomic bombs on us but that we may allow a world situation to develop in which ordinarily reasonable and humane men, acting as our representatives, may use such weapons in our name. We ought to be resolved beforehand that no provocation, no temptation shall induce us to resort to the last dreadful alternative of war.

"May no young man ever again be faced with the choice between violating his conscience by cooperating in competitive mass slaughter or separating himself from those who, endeavoring to serve liberty, democracy, humanity, can find no better way than to conscript young men to kill.

"As the world community develops in peace, it will open up great untapped reservoirs in human nature. Like a spring released from pressure would be the response of a generation of young men and women growing up in an atmosphere of friendliness and security, in a world demanding their service, offering them comradeship, calling to all adventurous and forward-reaching natures.

"We are not asked to subscribe to any utopia or to believe in a perfect world just around the corner. We are asked to be patient with necessarily slow and groping advance on the road forward, and to be ready for each step ahead as it becomes practicable. We are asked to equip ourselves with courage, hope, readiness for hard work, and to cherish large and generous ideals."

—*EMILY GREENE BALCH*   *(1946)*

"This international service is not mere humanitarianism; it is not merely mopping up, cleaning up the world after war. It is aimed at creating peace by setting an example of a different way of international service. So our foreign relief is a means of rehabilitation and it is intended not merely to help the body but to help the spirit and to give men hope that there can be a peaceful world."

—*HENRY CADBURY,* representing the
American Friends Service Committee   *(1947)*

"Upon this basic truth all the principles and actions of the Society of Friends are founded. Each man is seen as having intrinsic value, and Christ is equally concerned for the other man as for me. We all become part of the divine family, and as such we are all responsible for one another, carrying our share of the shame when wrong is done and of the burden of suffering."

—*MARGARET BACKHOUSE*,
representing the Friends Service Council of
Great Britain   *(1947)*

"For Europe at least, peace is inevitable. It can be either the peace of the grave, the peace of the dead empires of the past, which lost their creative spirit and failed to adjust themselves to new conditions, or a new dynamic peace applying science in a great leap forward in the evolution of human society to a new age in which hunger, poverty, and preventible diseases will be eliminated from the earth—an age in which the people in every country will rise to a far higher level of intellectual and cultural well-being, an age in which 'iron curtains' will disappear and people, though intensely patriotic for their own country, will be able to travel freely as world citizens. That is the hope science sets before us."

—*JOHN BOYD-ORR*   *(1949)*

"I am not an old admiral receiving the last and most magnificent decoration of his life. It is a profound joy, a joy of the soul, like that of a mountaineer who, half way up, has just had a sudden glimpse of the path which will allow him to climb farther and better."

—*FATHER DOMINIQUE PIRE*   *(1958)*

"Now we are forced to eliminate from the world forever this vestige of prehistoric barbarism, this curse to the human race. We, you and I, are privileged to be alive during this extraordinary age, this unique epoch in the history of the world, the epoch of demarcation between the past millennia of war and suffering, and the future, the great future of peace, justice, morality, and human well-being. We are privileged to have the opportunity of contributing to the achievement of the goal of the abolition of war and its replacement by world law. I am confident that we shall succeed in this great task; that the world community will thereby be freed not only from the suffering caused by war but also, through the better use of the earth's resources, of the discoveries of scientists, and of the efforts of mankind, from hunger, disease, illiteracy, and fear; and that we shall in the course of time be enabled to build a world characterized by economic, political, and social justice for all human beings and a culture worthy of man's intelligence."

—*Linus Pauling* *(1962)*

"I accept this award today with an abiding faith in America and an audacious faith in the future of mankind. I refuse to accept despair as the final response to the ambiguities of history. I refuse to accept the idea that the 'isness' of man's present nature makes him morally incapable of reaching up for the eternal 'oughtness' that forever confronts him. I refuse to accept the idea that man is mere flotsam and jetsam in the river of life unable to influence the unfolding events which surround him."

—*Martin Luther King, Jr.* *(1964)*

"So we must fix our vision not merely on the negative expulsion of war, but upon the positive affirmation of peace. We must see that peace represents a sweet music, a cosmic melody that is far superior to the discords of war. Somehow we must transform the dynamics of the world power struggle from the negative nuclear arms race which no one can win to a positive contest to harness man's creative genius for the purpose of making peace and prosperity a reality for all of the nations of the world. In short, we must shift the arms race into a 'peace race.' If we have the will and determination to mount such a peace offensive, we will unlock hitherto tightly sealed doors of hope and transform our imminent cosmic elegy into a psalm of creative fulfillment."

—*MARTIN LUTHER KING, JR.* *(1964)*

"In my view the role of voluntary organizations is becoming more and more essential. They are the only bodies that will have the necessary independence and initiative to restore some faith and idealism in our world. They deserve a great deal more support and encouragement.

"If disarmament can be achieved it will be due to the untiring, selfless work of the non-governmental sector. This is what Alfred Nobel appreciated in his days. It is more urgent than ever now. The big powers are traveling on the dangerous road of armament. The signpost just ahead of us is 'Oblivion.' Can the march on this road be stopped? Yes, if public opinion uses the power it now has."

—*SEAN MACBRIDE* *(1974)*

"Other civilizations, including more 'successful' ones, should exist an infinite number of times on the 'preceding' and the 'following' pages of the Book of the Universe. Yet this should not minimize our sacred endeavors in this world of ours, where, like faint glimmers of light in the dark, we have emerged for a moment from the nothingness of dark unconsciousness of material existence. We must make good the demands of reason and create a life worthy of ourselves and of the goals we only dimly perceive."

—*ANDREI SAKHAROV* (1975)

"The poor are very wonderful people. One evening we went out and we picked up four people from the street. And one of them was in a most terrible condition—and I told the sisters: You take care of the other three, I take care of this one who looked worse. So I did for her all that my love can do. I put her in bed, and there was such a beautiful smile on her face. She took hold of my hand as she said just the words 'Thank you,' and she died.

"I could not help but examine my conscience before her, and I asked what would I say if I was in her place. And my answer was very simple. I would have tried to draw a little attention to myself, I would have said I am hungry, that I am dying, I am cold, I am in pain, or something, but she gave me much more—she gave me her grateful love. And she died with a smile on her face. As did that man whom we picked up from the drain, half eaten with worms, and we brought him to the home. 'I have lived like an animal in the street, but I am going to die like an angel, loved and cared for.' And it was so wonderful to see the greatness of that man who could speak like that, who could die like that without blaming anybody, without cursing anybody, without comparing anything. Like an angel—this is the greatness of our people. And that is why we believe what Jesus had said: I was hungry—I was naked— I was homeless—I was unwanted, unloved, uncared for—and you did it to me.

"I believe that we are not real social workers. We may be doing social work in the eyes of the people, but we are really contemplatives in the heart of the world. For we are touching the body of Christ twenty-four hours. . . . And I think that in our family we don't need bombs and guns, to destroy, to bring peace—just get together, love one another, bring that peace, that joy, that strength of presence of each other in the home. And we will be able to overcome all the evil that is in the world."

—*MOTHER TERESA   (1979)*

"And with this prize that I have received as a Prize of Peace, I am going to try to make the home for many people who have no home. Because I believe that love begins at home, and if we can create a home for the poor I think that more and more love will spread. And we will be able through this understanding love to bring peace, be the good news to the poor. The poor in our own family first, in our country and in the world. To be able to do this, our Sisters, our lives have to be woven with prayer. They have to be woven with Christ to be able to understand, to be able to share. Because to be woven with Christ is to be able to understand, to be able to share. Because today there is so much suffering. . . . When I pick up a person from the street, hungry, I give him a plate of rice, a piece of bread, I have satisfied. I have removed that hunger. But a person who is shut out, who feels unwanted, unloved, terrified, the person who has been thrown out from society—that poverty is so full of hurt and so unbearable, and I find that very difficult. . . . And so let us always meet each other with a smile, for the smile is the beginning of love, and once we begin to love each other naturally we want to do something."

—*MOTHER TERESA*   (1979)

"We live in hope because we believe, like St. Paul, that love never dies. Human beings in the historical process have created enclaves of love by their active practice of solidarity throughout the world, and with a view to the full-orbed liberation of peoples and all humanity.

"For me it is essential to have the inward peace and serenity of prayer in order to listen to the silence of God, which speaks to us, in our personal lives and in the history of our times, about the power of love.

"Because of our faith in Christ and humankind, we must apply our humble efforts to the construction of a more just and humane world. And I want to declare emphatically: *Such a world is possible.*

"To create this new society, we must present outstretched and friendly hands, without hatred and rancor, even as we show great determination and never waver in the defense of truth and justice. Because we know that we cannot sow seeds with clenched fists. To sow we must open our hands."

—*ADOLFO PÉREZ ESQUIVEL*   (1980)

"My voice would like to have the strength of the voice of the humble and lowly. It is a voice that denounces injustice and proclaims hope in God and humanity. For this hope is the hope of all human beings who yearn to live in communion with all persons as their brothers and sisters and as children of God."

—*ADOLFO PÉREZ ESQUIVEL* (*1980*)

"The prize has given fresh hope to many in a world that has sometimes had a pall of despondency cast over it by the experience of suffering, disease, poverty, famine, hunger, oppression, injustice, evil, and war. A pall that has made many wonder whether God cares, whether he was omnipotent, whether he was loving and compassionate."

—*DESMOND MPILO TUTU* (*1984*)

"New hope has sprung in the breast of many as a result of this prize: a mother watching her child starve in front of some homeland resettlement camp, or one whose flimsy plastic shelter was demolished by the authorities in the KTC squatters' camp in Cape Town; the man emasculated, who lived for eleven months in single-sex hostels; the student receiving an inferior education; the activist languishing in a consulate or a solitary confinement cell, being tortured because he thought he was human and wanted that God-given right recognized; the exile longing to kiss the soil of her much-loved motherland; the political prisoner watching the days of a life sentence go by like the drip of a faulty tap, imprisoned because he knew he was created by God not to have his human dignity and pride trodden underfoot. A new hope has been kindled in the breasts of the millions who are voiceless, oppressed, dispossessed, tortured by the powerful tyrants, lacking elementary human rights in Latin America, Southeast Asia, in the Far

East, many parts of Africa, and behind the Iron Curtain, who have their noses rubbed in the dust.

"How wonderful, how appropriate that this award is made today, December 10, Human Rights Day. It says more eloquently than anything else that this is God's world, and He is in charge; that our cause is a just cause; that we will obtain human rights across Africa and everywhere in the world; we shall be free in South Africa and everywhere in the world. . . .

"On behalf of all these for whom you have given new hope, a new cause for joy, I want to accept this award in a wholly representative capacity.

"I accept this prestigious award on behalf of my family, on behalf of the South African Council of Churches, on behalf of all in my motherland, on behalf of those committed to the cause of justice, peace, and reconciliation everywhere.

"If God be for us who can be against us?"

—*DESMOND MPILO TUTU* (1984)

"For the physician, whose role is to affirm life, optimism is a medical imperative. Even when the outcome is doubtful, a patient's hopeful attitude promotes well-being and frequently leads to recovery. Pessimism degrades the quality of life and jeopardizes the tomorrows yet to come. An affirmative world view is essential if we are to shape a more promising future.

"The American poet Langston Hughes urged:

Hold on to dreams
For if dreams die,
Life is a broken winged bird
And cannot fly.

"We must hold fast to the dream that reason will prevail. The world today is full of anguish and dread. As great as is the danger, still greater is the opportunity. If science and technology have catapulted us to the brink of extinction, the same ingenuity has brought humankind to the boundary of an age of abundance.

"Never before was it possible to feed all the hungry. Never before was it possible to shelter all the homeless. Never before was it possible to teach all the illiterates. Never before were we able to heal so many afflictions. For the first time science and medicine can diminish drudgery and pain.

"Only those who can see the invisible can do the impossible. But in order to do the impossible, in the words of Jonathan Schell, we ask 'not for our personal survival: we ask only that we be survived. We ask for assurance that when we die as individuals, as we know we must, mankind will live on.'

"If we are to succeed, this vision must possess millions of people. We must convince each generation that they are but transient passengers on this planet earth. It does not belong to them. They are not free to doom generations yet unborn. They are not at liberty to erase humanity's past nor dim its future. Only life itself can lay claim to sacred continuity. The magnitude of the danger and its imminence must bring the human family together in a common pursuit of peace denied throughout this century. On the threshold of a new millennium the achievement of world peace is no longer remote, for it is beckoned by the unleashing of the deepest spiritual forces embedded in humankind when threatened with extinction. The reason, the creativeness, and the courage that human beings possess foster an abiding faith that what humanity creates, humanity can and will control."

—DR. EVGENY CHAZOV, representing International Physicians for the Prevention of Nuclear War *(1985)*

"Hope is the strongest driving force for a people. Hope which brings about change, which produces new realities, is what opens man's road to freedom. Once hope has taken hold, courage must unite with wisdom. That is the only way of avoiding violence, the only way of maintaining the calm one needs to respond peacefully to offenses."

—*OSCAR ARIAS SÁNCHEZ*   *(1987)*

"History was not written by men who predicted failure, who gave up their dreams, who abandoned their principles, who allowed their laziness to put their intelligence to sleep."

—*OSCAR ARIAS SÁNCHEZ*   *(1987)*

"Seeing the size of the challenge, no wonder many are prey to discouragement; or that apocalyptic prophets abound, announcing the failures of the fight against poverty, proclaiming the immediate fall of the democracies, forecasting the futility of peacemaking efforts.

"I do not share this defeatism. I cannot accept that to be realistic means to tolerate misery, violence, and hate. I do not believe that the hungry man should be treated as subversive for expressing his suffering. I shall never accept that the law can be used to justify tragedy, to keep things as they are, to make us abandon our ideas of a different world. Law is the path of liberty, and must as such open the way to progress for everyone."

—*OSCAR ARIAS SÁNCHEZ*   *(1987)*

"I feel honored, humbled and deeply moved that you should give this important prize to a simple monk from Tibet. I am no one special. But I believe the prize is a recognition of the true value of altruism, love, compassion and nonviolence which I try to practice, in accordance with the teachings of the Buddha and the great sages of India and Tibet."

—*THE DALAI LAMA   (1989)*

"As a Buddhist monk, my concern extends to all members of the human family and, indeed, to all sentient beings who suffer. I believe all suffering is caused by ignorance. People inflict pain on others in the selfish pursuit of their happiness or satisfaction. Yet true happiness comes from a sense of inner peace and contentment, which in turn must be achieved through the cultivation of altruism, of love and compassion, and elimination of ignorance, selfishness and greed."

—*THE DALAI LAMA   (1989)*

"I believe all religions pursue the same goals, that of cultivating human goodness and bringing happiness to all human beings. Though the means might appear different, the ends are the same. As we enter the final decade of this century I am optimistic that the ancient values that have sustained mankind are today reaffirming themselves to prepare us for a kinder, happier twenty-first century."

—*THE DALAI LAMA   (1989)*

"It is my dream that the entire Tibetan plateau should become a free refuge where humanity and nature can live in peace and in harmonious balance. It would be a place where people from all over the world could come to seek the true meaning of peace within themselves, away from the tensions and pressures of much of the rest of the world. Tibet could indeed become a creative center for the promotion and development of peace."

—*THE DALAI LAMA* (1989)

"The quest for democracy in Burma is the struggle of a people to live whole, meaningful lives as free and equal members of the world community. It is part of the unceasing human endeavor to prove that the spirit of man can transcend the flaws of his own nature."

—*AUNG SAN SUU KYI* (1991)

"That is why I dream of the day when the relationship between the indigenous peoples and other peoples is strengthened; when they can combine their potentialities and their capabilities and contribute to make life on this planet less unequal."

—*RIGOBERTA MENCHU TUM* (1992)

"We live with the hope that as she battles to remake herself, South Africa will be like a microcosm of the new world that is striving to be born.

"This must be a world of democracy and respect for human rights, a world freed from the horrors of poverty, hunger, deprivation and ignorance, relieved of the threat and the scourge of civil wars and external aggression and unburdened of the great tragedy of millions forced to become refugees.

"The processes in which South Africa and Southern Africa as a whole are engaged, beckon and urge us all that we take this tide at the flood and make of this region a living example of what all people of conscience would like the world to be."

—*NELSON MANDELA* *(1993)*

"The greatest peace, I believe, is the peace which we derive from our faith in God Almighty; from certainty about our relationship with our Creator. Crises might beset us, battles might rage about us—but if we have faith and the certainty it brings, we will enjoy peace—the peace that surpasses all understanding."

—*FREDERIK W. DE KLERK* *(1993)*

"The new era which is dawning in our country, beneath the great southern stars, will lift us out of the silent grief of our past and into a future in which there will be opportunity and space for joy and beauty—for real and lasting peace."

—*FREDERIK W. DE KLERK* *(1993)*

"Moreover, time and again, history has succumbed to the Bible's immortal ideas. The message that the one, invisible God created Man in His image, and hence there are no higher and lower orders of man, has fused with the realization that morality is the highest form of wisdom and, perhaps, of beauty and courage too.

"Slings, arrows, and gas chambers can annihilate man, but cannot destroy human values, dignity, and freedom."

—*SHIMON PERES* *(1994)*

"We will pursue the course of peace with determination and fortitude.

"We will not let up.

"We will not give in.

"Peace will triumph over all our enemies, because the alternative is grimmer for us all.

"And we will prevail.

"We will prevail because we regard the building of peace as a great blessing for us, and for our children after us. We regard it as a blessing for our neighbors on all sides, and for our partners in this enterprise—the United States, Russia, Norway, and all mankind.

"We wake up every morning, now, as different people. Suddenly, peace. We see the hope in our children's eyes. We see the light in our soldiers' faces, in the streets, in the buses, in the fields.

"We must not let them down.

"We will not let them down."

—*YITZHAK RABIN* *(1994)*

"Human dignity is rooted and fulfilled in God Himself. Persons have been placed in society by God the Creator, but over and above this, each person is called to be united with Him as children of God and participating in God's happiness. Moreover, if this divine foundation and the hope for all eternal life are missing, human dignity is strongly damaged."

—*CARLOS FILIPE XIMENES BELO* *(1996)*

"I speak of these things as one who has the responsibility to bear witness to what I have seen and heard, to react to what I know to be true, to keep the flame of hope alive, to do what is possible to warm the earth for still another day."

— *CARLOS FILIPE XIMENES BELO* (1996)

"God's modest gifts of health and wisdom to me will always be put to the service of peace and justice not only for my country and people but also for the cause of peace, freedom, and democracy everywhere where my faint voice can be heard."

— *JOSÉ RAMOS-HORTA* (1996)

"Concluding with a story of renewed hope: a Soviet cosmonaut had gone into space a few months earlier on one of those record-breaking missions in space. When he was blasted off from somewhere in the Soviet Union he carried a passport and a nationality granted to him by the most feared military empire in the world. Once he completed his tour of duty for the pride of the socialist motherland he prepared the spacecraft for its return voyage to earth. But he no longer had a country to return to. The mighty empire had ceased to exist. He was forced to circle the earth a few days longer until people of good will on earth decided to which country he should go to. With this note, I will end with renewed hope that no matter the level of brute force used against us, our dreams will never die."

— *JOSÉ RAMOS-HORTA* (1996)

"In the past thirty years of our conflict there have been many moments of deep depression and outright horror. Many people wondered whether the words of W. B. Yeats might come true: 'Too long a sacrifice / Can make a stone of the heart.' Endlessly our people gathered their strength to face another day and they never stopped encouraging their leaders to find the courage to resolve this situation so that our children could look to the future with a smile of hope. This is indeed their prize and I am convinced that they understand it in that sense and would take strong encouragement from today's significance and it will powerfully strengthen our peace process."

—*JOHN HUME*   *(1998)*

"I remember what one of my patients said to me in Kigali: 'Ummera, ummera-sha.' It is a Rwandan saying that loosely translated, means 'courage, courage, my friend—find and let live your courage.' It was said to me in Kigali at our hospital, by a woman who was not just attacked with a machete, but her entire body rationally and systematically mutilated. Her ears had been cut off. And her face had been so carefully disfigured, that a pattern was obvious in the slashes. There were hundreds of women, children and men brought to the hospital that day, so many that we had to lay them out on the street. And in many cases, we operated on them then and there, as the gutters around the hospital literally ran red with blood. She was one among many—living an inhuman and simply indescribable suffering. We could do little more for her at that moment than stop the bleeding with a few necessary sutures. We were completely overwhelmed, and she knew that there were so many others. She knew and I knew that there were so many others. She said to me in the clearest voice I have ever heard 'Allez, allez. Ummera, ummera-sha.' 'Go, go, my friend; find and let live your courage.'"

—*JAMES ORBINSKI,* representing Médecins
Sans Frontières   *(1999)*

"Another faith is my belief in the justice of history. In 1980, I was sentenced to death by the military regime. For six months in prison, I awaited the execution day. Often, I shuddered with fear of death. But I would find calm in the fact of history that justice ultimately prevails. I was then, and am still, an avid reader of history. And I knew that in all ages, in all places, he who lives a righteous life dedicated to his people and humanity may not be victorious, may meet a gruesome end in his lifetime, but will be triumphant and honored in history; he who wins by injustice may dominate the present day, but history will always judge him to be a shameful loser. There can be no exception."

—*KIM DAE-JUNG* (2000)

"I thought often during my years in the White House of an admonition that we received in our small school in Plains, Georgia, from a beloved teacher, Miss Julia Coleman. She often said: 'We must adjust to changing times and still hold to unchanging principles.'

"When I was a young boy, this same teacher also introduced me to Leo Tolstoy's novel *War and Peace*. She interpreted that powerful narrative as a reminder that the simple human attributes of goodness and truth can overcome great power. She also taught us that an individual is not swept along on a tide of inevitability but can influence even the greatest human events....

"I am not here as a public official, but as a citizen of a troubled world who finds hope in a growing consensus that the generally accepted goals of society are peace, freedom, human rights, environmental quality, the alleviation of suffering, and the rule of law."

—*JIMMY CARTER* (2002)

"Despite theological differences, all great religions share common commitments that define our ideal secular relationships. I am convinced that Christians, Muslims, Buddhists, Hindus, Jews, and others can embrace each other in a common effort to alleviate human suffering and to espouse peace."

—*JIMMY CARTER (2002)*

"Industry and global institutions must appreciate that ensuring economic justice, equity, and ecological integrity are of greater value than profits at any cost.

"The extreme global inequities and prevailing consumption patterns continue at the expense of the environment and peaceful co-existence. The choice is ours.

"I would like to call on young people to commit themselves to activities that contribute toward achieving their long-term dreams. They have the energy and creativity to shape a sustainable future. To the young people I say, you are a gift to your communities and indeed the world. You are our hope and our future."

—*WANGARI MAATHAI (2004)*

"And lest we forget:

"There is no religion that was founded on intolerance—and no religion that does not value the sanctity of human life.

"Judaism asks that we value the beauty and joy of human existence.

"Christianity says we should treat our neighbors as we would be treated.

"Islam declares that killing one person unjustly is the same as killing all of humanity.

"Hinduism recognizes the entire universe as one family.

"Buddhism calls on us to cherish the oneness of all creation.

"Some would say that it is too idealistic to believe in a society based on tolerance and the sanctity of human life, where borders, nationalities, and ideologies are of marginal importance. To those I say, this is not idealism, but rather realism, because history has taught us that war rarely resolves our differences. Force does not heal old wounds; it opens new ones."

—*MOHAMED ELBARADEI (2005)*

"Grameen [Bank] has given me an unshakeable faith in the creativity of human beings. This has led me to believe that human beings are not born to suffer the misery of hunger and poverty.

"To me poor people are like bonsai trees. When you plant the best seed of the tallest tree in a flower-pot, you get a replica of the tallest tree, only inches tall. There is nothing wrong with the seed you planted, only the soil-base that is too inadequate. Poor people are bonsai people. There is nothing wrong in their seeds. Simply, society never gave them the base to grow on. All it needs to get the poor people out of poverty is for us to create an enabling environment for them. Once the poor can unleash their energy and creativity, poverty will disappear very quickly.

"Let us join hands to give every human being a fair chance to unleash their energy and creativity."

—*MUHAMMAD YUNUS (2006)*

Elie Wiesel praying at the Unknown Jewish Martyr's Memorial in Paris (1987).

THE
TRAGEDY
OF
WAR

"One day . . . I watched, from the windows of my home, three Austrian soldiers fall amid a hail of bullets. Apparently dead, they were carried away to a neighboring square. I saw them again two hours later: one of them was still in the throes of dying. This sight froze the blood in my veins and I was overcome by a great compassion. In these three soldiers I no longer saw enemies, but men like myself, and with remorse as keenly suffered as if I had killed them with my own hands, I thought of their families, who were perhaps at that very moment preparing for their return.

"In that instant I felt all the cruelty and inhumanity of war which sets peoples against one another to their mutual detriment, peoples who should have every interest in understanding and being friends with each other. I was to feel this way many times as I looked at the dead and the wounded in all the wars for our independence in which I took part."

—*ERNESTO TEODORO MONETA* *(1907)*

"In the Capitoline Museum in Rome is a sculpture in marble which, in its simple pathos, seems to me to be a most beautiful creation. It is the statue of the 'Dying Gaul.' He is lying on the battlefield, mortally wounded. The vigorous body, hardened by work and combat, is sinking into death. The head, with its coarse hair, is bowed, the strong neck bends, the rough powerful workman's hand, till recently wielding the sword, now presses against the ground in a last effort to hold up the drooping body.

"He was driven to fight for foreign gods whom he did not know, far from his country. And thus he met his fate. Now he lies there, dying in silence. The noise of the fray no longer reaches his ear. His dimmed eyes are turned inward, perhaps on a final vision of his childhood home, where life was simple and happy, of his birthplace deep in the forest of Gaul.

"That is how I see mankind in its suffering; that is how I see the suffering people of Europe, bleeding to death on deserted battlefields after conflicts which to a great extent were not their own.

"This is the outcome of the lust for power, the imperialism, the militarism, that have run amok across the earth."

—*FRIDTJOF NANSEN* *(1922)*

"Let us face squarely the paradox that the world which goes to war is a world, usually, genuinely desiring peace. War is the outcome, not mainly of evil intentions, but on the whole, of good intentions which miscarry or are frustrated. It is made, not usually by evil men knowing themselves to be wrong, but is the outcome of policies pursued by good men usually passionately convinced that they are right."

—*NORMAN ANGELL* *(1933)*

"Who, indeed, could be so unseeing as not to realize that in modern war victory is illusory; that the harvest of war can be only misery, destruction, and degradation?

"If war should come, the peoples of the world would again be called upon to fight it, but they would not have willed it.

"Statesmen and philosophers repeatedly have warned that some values—freedom, honor, self-respect—are higher than peace or life itself. This may be true. Certainly, very many would hold that the loss of human dignity and self-respect, the chains of enslavement, are too high a price even for peace. But the horrible realities of modern warfare scarcely afford even this fatal choice. There is only suicidal escape, not freedom, in the death and destruction of atomic war. This is mankind's great dilemma. The well-being and the hopes of the peoples of the world can never be served until peace—as well as freedom, honor and self-respect—is secure."

—*RALPH J. BUNCHE* (1950)

"Throughout the ages . . . man has but little heeded the advice of the wise men. He has been—fatefully, if not willfully—less virtuous, less constant, less rational, less peaceful than he knows how to be, than he is fully capable of being. He has been led astray from the ways of peace and brotherhood by his addiction to concepts and attitudes of narrow nationalism, racial and religious bigotry, greed and lust for power. Despite this, despite the almost continuous state of war to which bad human relations have condemned him, he has made steady progress. In his scientific genius, man has wrought material miracles and has transformed his world. He has harnessed nature and has developed great civilizations. But he has never learned very well how to live with himself. The values he has created have been predominantly materialistic; his spiritual values have lagged far behind. He has demonstrated little spiritual genius and has made little progress toward the realization of human brotherhood. In the contemporary atomic age, this could prove man's fatal weakness.

"Alfred Nobel, a half-century ago, foresaw with prophetic vision that if the complacent mankind of his day could, with equanimity, contemplate war, the day would soon inevitably come when man would be confronted with the fateful alternative of peace or reversion to the Dark Ages. Man may well ponder whether he has not now reached that stage. Man's inventive genius has so far outstretched his reason—not his capacity to reason but his willingness to apply reason—that the peoples of the world find themselves precariously on the brink of total disaster."

—Ralph J. Bunche (1950)

"But the essential fact which we should acknowledge in our conscience, and which we should have acknowledged a long time ago, is that we are becoming inhuman to the extent that we become supermen. We have learned to tolerate the facts of war: that men are killed en masse—some twenty million in the Second World War—that whole cities and their inhabitants are annihilated by the atomic bomb, that men are turned into living torches by incendiary bombs. We learn of these things from the radio or newspapers and we judge them according to whether they signify success for the group of peoples to which we belong, or for our enemies. When we do admit to ourselves that such acts are the results of inhuman conduct, our admission is accompanied by the thought that the very fact of war itself leaves us no option but to accept them. In resigning ourselves to our fate without a struggle, we are guilty of inhumanity.

"What really matters is that we should all of us realize that we are guilty of inhumanity. The horror of this realization should shake us out of our lethargy so that we can direct our hopes and our intentions to the coming of an era in which war will have no place. This hope and this will can have but one aim: to attain, through a change in spirit, that superior reason which will dissuade us from misusing the power at our disposal."

—Albert Schweitzer (1952)

"There has been considerable comment over the awarding of the Nobel Peace Prize to a soldier. I am afraid this does not seem as remarkable to me as it quite evidently appears to others. I know a great deal of the horrors and tragedies of war. Today, as chairman of the American Battle Monuments Commission, it is my duty to supervise the construction and maintenance of military cemeteries in many countries overseas. . . . The cost of war in human lives is constantly spread before me, written neatly in many ledgers whose columns are gravestones. I am deeply moved to find some means or method of avoiding another calamity of war."

—*GEORGE C. MARSHALL* (1953)

"Today, less than ever, can we defend ourselves by force, for there is no effective defense against the all-destroying effect of nuclear missile weapons. Indeed, their very power has made their use intolerable, even unthinkable, because of the annihilative retaliation in kind that such use would invoke. So peace remains, as the phrase goes, balanced uneasily on terror, and the use of maximum force is frustrated by the certainty that it will be used in reply with a totally devastating effect. Peace, however, must surely be more than this trembling rejection of universal suicide.

"The stark and inescapable fact is that today we cannot defend our society by war since total war is total destruction, and if war is used as an instrument of policy, eventually we will have total war. Therefore, the best defense of peace is not power, but the removal of the causes of war, and international agreements which will put peace on a stronger foundation than the terror of destruction."

—*LESTER B. PEARSON* (1957)

"No dispute between nations can justify nuclear war. There is no defense against nuclear weapons that could not be overcome by increasing the scale of the attack. It would be contrary to the nature of war for nations to adhere to agreements to fight 'limited' wars, using only 'small' nuclear weapons—even little wars today are perilous, because of the likelihood that a little war would grow into a world catastrophe."

—*LINUS PAULING* *(1962)*

"I am intentionally not using the phrase 'striving for peace' too frequently. The longing for peace is rooted in the hearts of all men. But the striving, which at present has become so insistent, cannot lay claim to leading the way to eternal peace, or solving all disputes among nations, so strong are the economic and political roots. Nor can it create a lasting state of harmonious understanding between men. Our immediate striving must be aimed at preventing what, in the present situation, is the greatest threat to the very survival of mankind, the nuclear threat."

—*ALVA REIMER MYRDAL* *(1982)*

"The world, generally speaking, is now drifting on a more and more devastating course towards one single and absurd target of extermination—or rather, to be more exact—the northern hemisphere's towns, fields, and the people who have developed our civilization.

"The distressing situation of our age, which recalls the fate that overtook Rome, conceals—together with political and economic factors—a clearly irredeemable misconception, viz. that the use of weapons of war, *violence,* can lead to *victory.*

"Would it be possible, at immense expense, to inaugurate a new and happy existence for the world on the ruins of one that would be at least half-destroyed? The misconception that 'a victory is worth the price' has in the nuclear age become a total illusion."

—*ALVA REIMER MYRDAL*   *(1982)*

"The experts have as a rule arrived at the conclusion that the target for a sufficient deterrent would involve something like 400 missiles, capable of reaching from one continent to the other. Any developments over and above this have simply meant one more step in the direction of increased instability. It has been unnecessary, and at what a cost! . . .

"I shall go on repeating, until the politicians get it into their heads, that 'when one has enough, one does not need more.'"

—*ALVA REIMER MYRDAL*   *(1982)*

"I am convinced that today is a great and exciting day not only for the members of our international movement but also for all physicians on our planet, irrespective of their political and religious beliefs. For the first time in history, their selfless service for the cause of maintaining life on earth is marked by the high Nobel Prize. True to the Hippocratic Oath, we cannot keep silent knowing what the final epidemic—nuclear war—can bring to humankind. The bell of Hiroshima rings in our hearts not as a funeral knell but as an alarm bell calling out to actions to protect life on our planet."

—DR. EVGENY CHAZOV, representing
International Physicians for the Prevention of
Nuclear War   (1985)

"In our medical practice when we deal with a critical patient, in order to save him we mobilize all our energies and knowledge, sacrifice part of our hearts, enlist the cooperation of our most experienced colleagues. Today we face seriously ill humanity torn apart by distrust and fear of nuclear war. To save it we must arouse the conscience of the world's peoples, cultivate hate for nuclear weapons, repudiate egoism and chauvinism, create a favorable atmosphere of trust. In the nuclear age we are all interdependent. The earth is our only common home, which we cannot abandon. The new suicidal situation calls for the new thinking. We must convince those who make political decisions of this.

"Our professional duty is to protect life on earth. True to the Hippocratic Oath, physicians will dedicate their knowledge, their hearts and their lives to the happiness of their patients and well-being of the peoples of the world."

—DR. EVGENY CHAZOV, representing
International Physicians for the Prevention of
Nuclear War   (1985)

"We Soviet physicians, who know what a devastating war is like, not from history textbooks but from our own experience, who, together with all our people filled with hatred for war— we were troubled by the indifference demonstrated by many towards these irresponsible statements justifying the nuclear arms race. It was necessary to arouse the indifferent and turn them into active opponents of nuclear weapons. It was not simply our obligation as honest men, it was our professional duty. As Hippocrates said: 'The physician must inform the patient about everything that threatens his life.'"

—DR. EVGENY CHAZOV, representing
International Physicians for the Prevention of
Nuclear War   (1985)

"Physicians have demonstrated to the whole world that not only would nuclear war spell the end of civilization, it would also prejudice the existence of life on earth. My conscience— and I am sure the same applies to many of my colleagues in IPPNW—was staggered, primarily not by the total number of victims in nuclear war. The human mind finds it difficult to comprehend the figure of 2000 million victims. As they say, one death is death, but a million deaths are statistics. For us physicians, life is the aim of our work and each death is a tragedy. As people constantly involved in the care of patients, we felt the urge to warn governments and peoples that the critical point has been passed: medicine will be unable to render even minimal assistance to the victims of a nuclear conflict—the wounded, the burned, the sick—including the population of the country which unleashes nuclear war."

—DR. EVGENY CHAZOV, representing
International Physicians for the Prevention of
Nuclear War   (1985)

"This build-up is like a cancer, the cells of which multiply because they have been genetically programmed to do no other. Pointing nuclear-tipped missiles at entire nations is an unprecedented act of moral depravity. The horror is obscured by its magnitude, by the sophistication of the means of slaughter, and by the aseptic Orwellian language crafted to describe the attack— 'delivery vehicles' promote an 'exchange' in which the death of untold millions is called 'collateral damage.' Bertrand Russell called attention to the ethical bankruptcy that afflicts this era: 'Our world has sprouted a weird concept of security and a warped sense of morality. Weapons are sheltered like treasures while children are exposed to incineration.'"

—*DR. BERNARD LOWN*, representing
International Physicians for the Prevention of
Nuclear War *(1985)*

"Nothing provokes so much horror and opposition within the Jewish tradition as war. Our abhorrence of war is reflected in the paucity of our literature of warfare. After all, God created the Torah to do away with iniquity, to do away with war. Warriors fare poorly in the Talmud: Judas Maccabaeus is not even mentioned; Bar-Kochba is cited, but negatively. David, a great warrior and conqueror, is not permitted to build the Temple; it is his son Solomon, a man of peace, who constructs God's dwelling place. Of course some wars may have been necessary or inevitable, but none was ever regarded as holy. For us, a holy war is a contradiction in terms. War dehumanizes, war diminishes, war debases all those who wage it.

The Talmud says, *'Talmidei hakhamim shermarbin shalom baolam'* (It is the wise men who will bring about peace)."

—ELIE WIESEL (1986)

"We must remember the suffering of my people, as we must remember that of the Ethiopians, the Cambodians, the boat people, the Palestinians, the Mesquite Indians, the Argentinian desaparecidos—the list seems endless.

"Let us remember Job, who, having lost everything—his children, his friends, his possessions, and even his argument with God—still found the strength to begin again, to rebuild his life. Job was determined not to repudiate the creation, however imperfect, that God had entrusted to him."

—ELIE WIESEL (1986)

"The world today is divided between those who live in fear of being destroyed in nuclear war, and those who are dying day by day in wars fought with conventional weapons. This terror of the final war is so great that it has spread the most frightening insensibility towards the arms race and the use of non-nuclear weapons. We need most urgently—our intelligence requires us, our pity enjoins us—to struggle with equal intensity to ensure that neither Hiroshima nor Vietnam is repeated."

—OSCAR ARIAS SÁNCHEZ (1987)

"However noble a crusade, some people will desire and promote its failure. Some few appear to accept war as the normal course of events, as the solution to problems. How ironic that powerful forces are angered by interruptions in the course of war, by efforts to eliminate the sources of hatred! How ironic that any intention to stop war in its course triggers rages and attacks, as if we were disturbing the sleep of the just or halting a necessary measure, and not a heart-rending evil! How ironic for peacemaking efforts to discover that hatred is stronger for many than love; that the longing to achieve power through military victories makes so many men lose their reason, forget all shame, and betray history."

—*OSCAR ARIAS SÁNCHEZ (1987)*

"Hundreds of cemeteries in our part of the Middle East—in our home in Israel—but also in Egypt, in Syria, Jordan, Lebanon, and Iraq. From the plane's window, from thousands of feet above them, the countless tombstones are silent. But the sound of their outcry has carried from the Middle East throughout the world for decades.

"Standing here today, I wish to salute loved ones—and foes. I wish to salute all the fallen of all the countries in all the wars; the members of their families who bear the enduring burden of bereavement; the disabled whose scars will never heal. Tonight I wish to pay tribute to each and every one of them, for this important prize is theirs, and theirs alone."

—*YITZHAK RABIN (1994)*

"As a military man, as a commander, I issued orders for dozens, probably hundreds of military operations. And together with the joy of victory and grief of bereavement, I shall always remember the moment just after taking the decision to mount an action: the hush as senior officers or cabinet ministers slowly rise from their seats; the sight of their receding backs; the sound of the closing door; and then the silence in which I remain alone.

"That is the moment you grasp that as a result of the decision just made, people will be going to their deaths. People from my nation, people from other nations. And they still don't know it.

"At that hour, they are still laughing and weeping; still weaving plans and dreaming about love; still musing about planting a garden or building a house—and they have no idea these are their last hours on earth. Which of them is fated to die? Whose picture will appear in a black border in tomorrow's newspaper? Whose mother will soon be in mourning? Whose world will crumble under the weight of the loss?

"In that moment of great tension just before the finger pulls the trigger, just before the fuse begins to burn; in the terrible quiet of that moment, there's still time to wonder, alone: Is it really imperative to act? Is there no other choice? No other way?

"And then the order is given, and the inferno begins."

—*YITZHAK RABIN*   *(1994)*

"War must cease to be an admissible social institution. We must learn to resolve our disputes by means other than military confrontation. This need was recognized forty years ago when we said in the Russell-Einstein Manifesto: 'Here then is the problem which we present to you, stark and dreadful and inescapable: shall we put an end to the human race; or shall mankind renounce war?'"

—*JOSEPH ROTBLAT*   *(1995)*

"Land mines, torture equipment, cluster bombs, chemical weapons are weapons designed to inflict pain and death on human beings. Most victims are civilians, women and children. How can arms manufacturers, weapons designers, plant managers, politicians, who have families of their own whom they love, be so insensitive when it comes to the suffering of other human beings?"

—JOSÉ RAMOS-HORTA   (1996)

"Landmines distinguish themselves because once they have been sown, once the soldier walks away from the weapon, the landmine cannot tell the difference between a soldier or a civilian—a woman, a child, a grandmother going out to collect firewood to make the family meal. The crux of the problem is that while the use of the weapon might be militarily justifiable during the day of the battle, or even the two weeks of the battle, or maybe even the two months of the battle, once peace is declared the landmine does not recognize that peace. The landmine is eternally prepared to take victims. In common parlance, it is the perfect soldier, the 'eternal sentry.' The war ends, the landmine goes on killing."

—JODY WILLIAMS   (1997)

"The lesson of the past century has been that where the dignity of the individual has been trampled or threatened—where citizens have not enjoyed the basic right to choose their government, or the right to change it regularly—conflict has too often followed, with innocent civilians paying the price, in lives cut short and communities destroyed."

—KOFI ANNAN (2001)

"In order for us human beings to commit ourselves personally to the inhumanity of war, we find it necessary first to dehumanize our opponents, which is in itself a violation of the beliefs of all religions. Once we characterize our adversaries as beyond the scope of God's mercy and grace, their lives lose all value. We deny personal responsibility when we plant landmines and, days or years later, a stranger to us—often a child—is crippled or killed. From a great distance, we launch bombs or missiles with almost total impunity, and never want to know the number or identity of the victims."

—*JIMMY CARTER (2002)*

"Consider also our approach to the sanctity and value of human life. In the aftermath of the September 2001 terrorist attacks in the United States, we all grieved deeply, and expressed outrage at this heinous crime—and rightly so. But many people today are unaware that, as the result of civil war in the Democratic Republic of the Congo, 3.8 million people have lost their lives since 1998.

"Are we to conclude that our priorities are skewed, and our approaches uneven?"

—*MOHAMED ELBARADEI (2005)*

"We still have eight or nine countries who possess nuclear weapons. We still have 27,000 warheads in existence. I believe this is 27,000 too many."

—*MOHAMED ELBARADEI (2005)*

"Indeed, without realizing it, we have begun to wage war on the earth itself. Now, we and the earth's climate are locked in a relationship familiar to war planners: 'Mutually assured destruction.'

"More than two decades ago, scientists calculated that nuclear war could throw so much debris and smoke into the air that it would block life-giving sunlight from our atmosphere, causing a 'nuclear winter.' Their eloquent warnings here in Oslo helped galvanize the world's resolve to halt the nuclear arms race.

"Now science is warning us that if we do not quickly reduce the global warming pollution that is trapping so much of the heat our planet normally radiates back out of the atmosphere, we are in danger of creating a permanent 'carbon summer.'

"As the American poet Robert Frost wrote, 'Some say the world will end in fire; some say in ice.' Either, he notes, 'would suffice.'

"But neither need be our fate. It is time to make peace with the planet."

—AL GORE, JR. (2007)

Martin Luther King, Jr. (center, with button on lapel), *marching in Boston with Ralph Abernathy* (right) *and the Reverend Virgil Wood* (1965).

VIOLENCE
AND
NONVIOLENCE

"I believe the greatest risk of war is in the minds of men who have an unrepentant and unchanging view of the justification of past wars. So perhaps in a world like this there is room for a few thousand persons like Quakers, who take the opposite view, who begin with the assumption that war is not and has not been and will not be justified, on either practical or moral grounds."

—*HENRY J. CADBURY,* representing the
American Friends Service Committee   *(1947)*

"That does not mean that wars are not waged for just ends. It means that we do not believe that it is the only way to achieve those just ends. We believe the means are not consistent with the ends, and the better the ends for which men fight, the less moral, the less effective is the method of war. In this particular area, mankind falls behind the standard we have accepted elsewhere. So on this point the Quaker is not an unrealistic perfectionist, but a practical moralist. He believes that this problem can be solved by other means. He believes this problem of war is a moral problem and that the force of religion is essential to its solution. The nature of religion on the one hand and the task of abolishing war on the other seem to us to fit perfectly with each other as task and tool should fit. Religion is concerned with the spiritual life of man. The elimination of war is a spiritual problem and so no wonder we cling in all states of our religious development to this viewpoint."

—*HENRY J. CADBURY,* representing the
American Friends Service Committee   *(1947)*

"It has come to us first as individuals—what shall I do, what is my duty? If an individual thinks that war is evil, we are so simple-minded, so naive, as to say: 'If war is evil, then I do not take part in it,' just as one might say, if drunkenness is evil, then I do not drink; if slaveholding is evil, then I do not hold slaves. I know that sounds too simple—almost foolish. I admit that that is our point of view, and this means, of course, that in every war some Friends have suffered not only fines, torture, punishment, or exile, but even the threat of death, which, of course, is no more than the soldier faces, but in a different cause. . . . We recognize that there are times when resistance appears at first to be a real virtue, and then only those most deeply rooted in religious pacifism can resist by other than physical means. We have learned that in the end the spirit can conquer evil and we believe that in many recent situations those who have unwillingly employed force have learned this lesson at the last."

—*HENRY H. CADBURY,* representing the
American Friends Service Committee   *(1947)*

"I accept the Nobel Prize for Peace at a moment when 22 million Negroes of the United States of America are engaged in a creative battle to end the long night of racial injustice. I accept this award on behalf of a civil rights movement which is moving with determination and a majestic scorn for risk and danger to establish a reign of freedom and a rule of justice. I am mindful that only yesterday in Birmingham, Alabama, our children, crying out for brotherhood, were answered with fire hoses, snarling dogs and even death. I am mindful that only yesterday in Philadelphia, Mississippi, young people seeking to secure the right to vote were brutalized and murdered. And only yesterday more than forty houses of worship in the state of Mississippi alone were bombed or burned because they offered a sanctuary to those who would not accept segregation. I am mindful that debilitating and grinding poverty afflicts my people and chains them to the lowest rung of the economic ladder.

"Therefore, I must ask why this prize is awarded to a movement which is beleaguered and committed to unrelenting struggle: to a movement which has not won the very peace and brotherhood which is the essence of the Nobel Prize.

"After contemplation, I conclude that this award which I receive on behalf of that movement is a profound recognition that nonviolence is the answer to the crucial political and moral question of our time—the need for man to overcome oppression and violence without resorting to violence and oppression. Civilization and violence are antithetical concepts. Negroes of the United States, following the people of India, have demonstrated that nonviolence is not sterile passivity, but a powerful moral force which makes for social transformation. Sooner or later all the peoples of the world will have to discover a way to live together in peace, and thereby transform this pending cosmic elegy into a creative psalm of brotherhood. If this is to be achieved man must evolve for all human conflict a method which rejects revenge, aggression and retaliation. The foundation of such a method is love."

—*MARTIN LUTHER KING, JR.*   *(1964)*

"The word that symbolizes the spirit and the outward form of our encounter is nonviolence, and it is doubtless that factor which made it seem appropriate to award a peace prize to one identified with struggle. Broadly speaking, nonviolence in the civil rights struggle has meant not relying on arms and weapons of struggle. It has meant non-cooperation with customs and laws which are institutional aspects of a regime of discrimination and enslavement. . . .

"Nonviolence has also meant that my people in the agonizing struggles of recent years have taken suffering upon themselves instead of inflicting it on others."

—*MARTIN LUTHER KING, JR.* *(1964)*

"In a real sense nonviolence seeks to redeem the spiritual and moral lag [that I spoke of earlier] as the chief dilemma of modern man. It seeks to secure moral ends through moral means. Nonviolence is a powerful and just weapon. Indeed, it is a weapon unique in history, which cuts without wounding and ennobles the man who wields it."

—*MARTIN LUTHER KING, JR.* *(1964)*

"We as Peace People go much further: we believe in taking down the barriers, but we also believe in the most energetic reconciliation among peoples by getting them to know each other, talk each other's languages, understand each other's fears and beliefs, getting to know each other physically, philosophically, and spiritually. It is much harder to kill your near neighbor than the thousands of unknown and hostile aliens at the other end of a nuclear missile. We have to create a world in which there are no unknown, hostile aliens at the other end of any missiles, and that is going to take a tremendous amount of sheer hard work.

"The only force which can break down those barriers is the force of love, the force of truth, soul-force. . . .

"We are deeply, passionately dedicated to the cause of nonviolence, to the force of truth and love, to soul-force. To those who say that we are naive, utopian idealists, we say that we are the only realists, and that those who continue to support militarism in our time are supporting the progress towards total self-destruction of the human race, when the only right and left will be dead to the right and dead to the left, and death and destruction right, left and center, east and west, north and south.

"We wish to see those who keep the lights burning twenty-four hours a day in the Pentagon and the Kremlin and all the other great centers of militarism liberated into truly creative and happy lives instead of the soul-destroying tasks of preparing for self-destruction."

—BETTY WILLIAMS (1976)

"I want to receive this distinction in the name of the people of Latin America and, in a very special way, in the name of the poorest and smallest of my brothers and sisters because they are the most beloved of God. I receive it in the name of my indigenous brothers and sisters, the peasants, workers, and young people—in the name of the thousands of members of religious orders and of men and women of goodwill who relinquish their privileges to share the life and path of the poor, and who struggle to build a new society.

"For a man like myself—a small voice for those who have no voice—who struggles so that the cry of the people may be heard in all its power; for one without any identifying affiliation other than as a flesh-and-blood Latin American and as a Christian, this is, without any doubt, the highest honor that I can receive, which is to be considered a servant of peace.

"I come from a continent that lives between anguish and hope. For this continent where I live, the choice of the evangelical power of nonviolence presents itself, I am convinced, as a challenge that opens up new and radical perspectives.

"It is a choice that gives priority to a value essentially and profoundly Christian—the dignity of the human being, the sacred, transcendent, and irrevocable dignity that belongs to the human being by reason of being a child of God and a brother or sister in Christ, and therefore our own brother and sister."

—*ADOLFO PÉREZ ESQUIVEL* (1980)

"Because war and preparations for war have acquired legitimacy, and because of the tremendous proliferation of arms through production and export, so that they are now available more or less to all and sundry, right down to handguns and stilettoes, the cult of violence has by now so permeated relations between people that we are compelled to witness as well an increase in everyday violence."

—*ALVA REIMER MYRDAL* (1982)

"War is murder. And the military preparations now being made for a potential major conflict are aimed at collective murder. In a nuclear age the victims would be numbered by the millions.

"The naked truth of this must be faced.

"The age in which we live can only be described as one of barbarism. Our civilization is in the process not only of being militarized, but also of being brutalized.

"There are two main features characteristic of this senseless trend: *rivalry* and *violence.* Rivalry for the power to exploit the headlong onrush of technology militates against cooperation, and results in increasing violence, with more and more sophisticated weapons being used. This is precisely what marks our age as one of barbarism and brutalization. But the moment of truth should now have arrived.

"I know that these are strong words. I know, too, that there are good forces at work trying to check this ill-starred development.

"May I at this juncture make a personal confession? I have always regarded global development as a struggle between good and evil forces. Not, to put it simply, a struggle between Jesus and Satan, since I do not consider that the development is restricted to our own sphere of culture. Rather perhaps a struggle between Ormuzd, the good, and Ahriman, the evil. My personal philosophy of life is *ethics*.

"It seems to me as if the evil forces have concentrated more and more power in their hands. Dare we believe that the leaders of the world's great nations will wake up, will see the precipice towards which they are moving, and *change direction?*"

—*ALVA REIMER MYRDAL* *(1982)*

"When I recall my own path of life I cannot but speak of the violence, hatred and lies. A lesson drawn from such experiences, however, was that we can effectively oppose violence only if we ourselves do not resort to it."

—*LECH WAŁESA* *(1983)*

"Never before in history have military forces been employed internationally *not* to wage war, *not* to establish domination, and *not* to serve the interests of any power or group of powers, but rather to prevent conflict between peoples."

—*JAVIER PÉREZ DE CUÉLLAR,* representing the United Nations Peace-Keeping Forces *(1988)*

"The suffering of our people during the past forty years of occupation is well documented. Ours has been a long struggle. We know our cause is just. Because violence can only breed more violence and suffering, our struggle must remain nonviolent and free of hatred. We are trying to end the suffering of our people, not to inflict suffering upon others."

—*THE DALAI LAMA* (1989)

"The quest for a war-free world has a basic purpose: survival. But if in the process we learn how to achieve it by love rather than by fear, by kindness rather than by compulsion; if in the process we learn to combine the essential with the enjoyable, the expedient with the benevolent, the practical with the beautiful, this will be an extra incentive to embark on this great task."

—*JOSEPH ROTBLAT* (1995)

"The world censures those who take up arms to defend their causes and calls on them to use nonviolent means in voicing their grievances. But when a people chooses the nonviolent path, it is all too often the case that hardly anyone pays attention. It is tragic that people have to suffer and die and the television cameras have to deliver the pictures to people's homes every day before the world at large admits there is a problem."

—*CARLOS FILIPE XIMENES BELO* (1996)

"Throughout my years in political life, I have seen extraordinary courage and fortitude by individual men and women, innocent victims of violence. Amid shattered lives, a quiet heroism has borne silent rebuke to the evil that violence represents, to the carnage and waste of violence, to its ultimate futility."

—*JOHN HUME* (1998)

Andrei Sakharov participating in a protest against the Soviet Academy of Sciences (1989).

HUMAN
RIGHTS

"It is worthy of emphasis that the United Nations exists not merely to preserve the peace but also to make change—even radical change—possible without violent upheaval. The United Nations has no vested interest in the status quo. It seeks a more secure world, a better world, a world of progress for all peoples. In the dynamic world society which is the objective of the United Nations, all peoples must have equality and equal rights."

—*RALPH J. BUNCHE*   *(1950)*

"The United Nations stands for the freedom and equality of all peoples, irrespective of race, religion, or ideology. It is for the peoples of every society to make their own choices with regard to ideologies, economic systems, and the relationship which is to prevail between the state and the individual. The United Nations is engaged in an historic effort to underwrite the rights of man. It is also attempting to give reassurance to the colonial peoples that their aspirations for freedom can be realized, if only gradually, by peaceful processes."

—*RALPH J. BUNCHE*   *(1950)*

"Whatever may be the future of our freedom efforts, our cause is the cause of the liberation of people who are denied freedom. Only on this basis can the peace of Africa and the world be firmly founded. Our cause is the cause of equality between nations and peoples. Only thus can the brotherhood of man be firmly established."

—*ALBERT JOHN LUTULI*   *(1960)*

"I did not initiate the struggle to extend the area of human freedom in South Africa; other African patriots—devoted men—did so before me. I also, as a Christian and patriot, could not look on while systematic attempts were made, almost in every department of life, to debase the God-factor in man or to set a limit beyond which the human being in his black form might not strive to serve his Creator to the best of his ability. To remain neutral in a situation where the laws of the land virtually criticized God for having created men of color was the sort of thing I could not, as a Christian, tolerate."

—*ALBERT JOHN LUTULI* *(1960)*

"The right of an individual to refuse to kill, to torture, or to participate in the preparation for the nuclear destruction of humanity seems to me to be fundamental."

—*SEAN MACBRIDE* *(1974)*

"I would like to end my speech expressing the hope in a final victory of the principles of peace and human rights. The best sign that such hope can come true would be a general political amnesty in all the world, liberation of all prisoners of conscience everywhere. The struggle for a general political amnesty is the struggle for the future of mankind.

"I am deeply grateful to the Nobel Committee for awarding me the Nobel Peace Prize for 1975 and I beg you to remember that the honor which was thus granted to me is shared by all prisoners of conscience in the Soviet Union and in other Eastern European countries as well as by all those who fight for their liberation."

—*ANDREI SAKHAROV* *(1975)*

"I am convinced that international confidence, mutual understanding, disarmament, and international security are inconceivable without an open society with freedom of information, freedom of conscience, the right to publish, and the right to travel and choose the country in which one wishes to live. I am likewise convinced that freedom of conscience, together with the other civic rights, provides the basis for scientific progress and constitutes a guarantee that scientific advances will not be used to despoil mankind, providing the basis for economic and social progress, which in turn is a political guarantee for the possibility of an effective defense of social rights. At the same time I should like to defend the thesis of the original and decisive significance of civic and political rights in molding the destiny of mankind. This view differs essentially from the widely accepted Marxist view, as well as the technocratic opinions, according to which it is precisely material factors and social and economic conditions that are of decisive importance."

—ANDREI SAKHAROV   (1975)

"Granting the award to a person who defends political and civil rights against illegal and arbitrary actions means an affirmation of principles which play such an important role in determining the future of mankind. For hundreds of people, known or unknown to me, many of whom pay a high price for the defense of these same principles (the price being loss of freedom, unemployment, poverty, persecution, exile from one's country), your decision was a great personal joy and a gift. I am aware of all this, but I am also aware of another fact: in the present situation, it is an act of intellectual courage and great equity to grant the award to a man whose ideas do not coincide with official concepts of the leadership of a big and powerful state. This, in fact, is how I value the decision of the Nobel Committee; I also see in it a manifestation of tolerance and of the true spirit of détente. I want to hope that even those who at present view your decision skeptically or with irritation someday will come to share this point of view."

—ANDREI SAKHAROV (1975)

"People everywhere need to be continually reminded that violations of human rights, whether arbitrary arrest and detention, unjust imprisonment, torture, or political assassination, are threats to world peace. Each violation, wherever it occurs, can set in motion a trend towards the debasement of human dignity. From individuals to groups, from groups to nations, from nations to groups of nations, in chain reaction a pattern sets in, a pattern of violence and repression and a lack of concern for human welfare.

"This must never be allowed to start. And the place to stop it is at the level of the individual. Therefore, the protection of the rights of the individual to think freely, to express himself freely, to associate freely with others and to disseminate his thoughts is essential to the preservation of world peace."

—MÜMTAZ SOYSAL, representing
Amnesty International *(1977)*

"We are accustomed to hear, wherever human rights are being violated, that this is being done in the name of higher interests.

"I declare that there exists no higher interest than the Human Being.

"I point out my conviction of the maturity of the people, who are able to govern themselves without paternalistic guardians.

"For this reason we have hope. Because we believe in the vocation of communion and participation of our people, who day to day awaken to their political conscience and express their desire for change and profound democratization of society. A change based on justice, built with love, and which will bring to us the most anxiously desired fruits of peace.

"We must all commit ourselves to this task. And I want my voice to help build the chorus of voices so that the clamor for justice will become deafening.

"I live in the hope which I surely share with many others. I am confident that one day our daily effort will have its reward."

—*ADOLFO PÉREZ ESQUIVEL (1980)*

"In many parts of the world the people are searching for a solution which would link the two basic values: peace and justice. The two are like bread and salt for mankind."

—*LECH WAŁESA (1983)*

"You are aware of the reasons why I could not come to your capital city and receive personally this distinguished prize. On that solemn day my place is among those with whom I have grown and to whom I belong—the workers of Gdansk.

"Let my words convey to you the joy and the never extin-guished hope of the millions of my brothers—the millions of working people in factories and offices, associated in the union whose very name expresses one of the noblest aspirations of humanity. Today all of them, like myself, feel greatly honored by the Prize. . . .

"For the first time a Pole has been awarded a prize which Alfred Nobel founded for activities towards bringing the nations of the world closer together.

"The most ardent hopes of my compatriots are linked with this idea—in spite of the violence, cruelty and brutality which characterize the conflicts splitting the present-day world.

"We desire peace—and that is why we have never resorted to physical force. We crave for justice—and that is why we are so persistent in the struggle for our rights. We seek freedom of convictions—and that is why we have never attempted to enslave man's conscience, nor shall we ever attempt to do so.

"We are fighting for the right of the working people to association and for the dignity of human labor. We respect the dignity and the rights of every man and every nation. The path to a brighter future of the world leads through honest reconciliation of the conflicting interests and not through hatred and bloodshed. To follow that path means to enhance the moral power of the all-embracing idea of human solidarity."

—*LECH WAŁESA*   *(1983)*

"One thing . . . must be said here and now on this solemn occasion: the Polish people have not been subjugated nor have they chosen the road of violence and fratricidal bloodshed.

"We shall not yield to violence. We shall not be deprived of union freedoms. We shall never agree with sending people to prison for their convictions. The gates of prisons must be thrown open and persons sentenced for defending union and civic rights must be set free. The announced trial of eleven leading members of our movement must never be held. All those already sentenced or still awaiting trials for their union activities or their convictions should return to their homes and be allowed to live and work in their country.

"The defense of our rights and our dignity, as well as efforts never to let ourselves be overcome by the feeling of hatred—this is the road we have chosen."

—*LECH WAŁESA*   *(1983)*

"When will we learn that human beings are of infinite value because they have been created in the image of God, and that it is a blasphemy to treat them as if they were less than this, and to do so ultimately recoils on those who do this? In dehumanizing others, they are themselves dehumanized. Perhaps oppression dehumanizes the oppressor as much as, if not more than, the oppressed. They need each other to become truly free to become human. We can be human only in fellowship, in community, in *koinonia,* in peace."

—*DESMOND MPILO TUTU* *(1984)*

"It is with a profound sense of humility that I accept the honor you have chosen to bestow upon me. I know: your choice transcends me. This both frightens and pleases me.

"It frightens me because I wonder: do I have the right to represent the multitudes who have perished? Do I have the right to accept this great honor on their behalf? . . . I do not. That would be presumptuous. No one may speak for the dead, no one may interpret their mutilated dreams and visions.

"It pleases me because I may say that this honor belongs to all the survivors and their children, and through us, to the Jewish people with whose destiny I have always identified."

—*ELIE WIESEL* *(1986)*

"I express to you my deepest gratitude. No one is as capable of gratitude as one who has emerged from the kingdom of night. We know that every moment is a moment of grace, every hour an offering; not to share them would mean to betray them. Our lives no longer belong to us alone; they belong to all those who need us desperately. . . .

"Thank you, people of Norway, for declaring on this singular occasion that our survival has meaning for mankind."

—*ELIE WIESEL* *(1986)*

"I swore never to be silent whenever and wherever human beings endure suffering and humiliation. We must always take sides. Neutrality helps the oppressor, never the victim. Silence encourages the tormentor, never the tormented. Sometimes we must interfere. When human lives are endangered, when human dignity is in jeopardy, national borders and sensitivities become irrelevant. Wherever men or women are persecuted because of their race, religion, or political views, that place must—at that moment—become the center of the universe."

—*ELIE WIESEL* *(1986)*

"There is much to be done, there is much that can be done. One person—a Raoul Wallenberg, an Albert Schweitzer, one person of integrity—can make a difference, a difference of life and death. As long as one dissident is in prison, our freedom will not be true. As long as one child is hungry, our lives will be filled with anguish and shame. What all these victims need above all is to know that they are not alone; that we are not forgetting them, that when their voices are stifled we shall lend them ours, that while their freedom depends on ours, the quality of our freedom depends on theirs."

—*ELIE WIESEL* *(1986)*

"Job, our ancestor. Job, our contemporary. His ordeal concerns all humanity. Did he ever lose his faith? If so, he rediscovered it within his rebellion. He demonstrated that faith is essential to rebellion, and that hope is possible beyond despair. The source of his hope was memory, as it must be ours. Because I remember, I despair. Because I remember, I have the duty to reject despair.

"I remember the killers, I remember the victims, even as I struggle to invent a thousand and one reasons to hope.

"There may be times when we are powerless to prevent injustice, but there must never be a time when we fail to protest. The Talmud tells us that by saving a single human being, man can save the world. We may be powerless to open all the jails and free all the prisoners, but by declaring our solidarity with one prisoner, we indict all jailers. None of us is in a position to eliminate war, but it is our obligation to denounce it and expose it in all its hideousness. . . . Mankind needs peace more than ever, for our entire planet, threatened by nuclear war, is in danger of total destruction. A destruction only man can provoke, only man can prevent.

"Mankind must remember that peace is not God's gift to his creatures, it is our gift to each other."

—*ELIE WIESEL* *(1986)*

"When you decided to honor me with this prize, you decided to honor a country of peace, you decided to honor Costa Rica. When, in this year 1987, you carried out the will of Alfred Nobel to encourage peace efforts in the world, you decided to encourage the efforts to secure peace in Central America. I am very grateful for the recognition of our search for peace. . . .

"To receive this Nobel Prize on the 10th of December is for me a marvelous coincidence. My son—here present—is eight years old today. I say to him, and through him to all the children of my country, that we shall never resort to violence, we shall never support military solutions to the problems of Central America. It is for the new generation that we must understand more than ever that this can only be achieved through its own instruments: dialogue and understanding, tolerance and forgiveness, freedom and democracy.

"I know well you share what we say to all members of the international community, and particularly to those both in the East and West with far greater power and resources than my small nation could ever hope to possess. I say to them with the utmost urgency, let Central Americans decide the future of Central America; leave interpretation, implementation of our peace plan to us. Support the efforts for peace instead of the forces of war in our region. Send our peoples ploughshares instead of swords, pruning hooks instead of shears. If they, for their own purposes, cannot refrain from amassing the weapons of war, then in the name of God, at least they should leave us in peace."

—*OSCAR ARIAS SÁNCHEZ* *(1987)*

"Costa Rica's fortress, the strength which makes it invincible by force, which makes it stronger than a thousand armies, is the power of liberty, of its principles, of the great ideals of our civilization."

—*OSCAR ARIAS SÁNCHEZ* *(1987)*

"As a free spokesman for my captive countrymen and -women, I feel it is my duty to speak out on their behalf. I speak not with a feeling of anger or hatred towards those who are responsible for the immense suffering of our people and the destruction of our land, homes and culture. They too are human beings who struggle to find happiness and deserve our compassion. I speak to inform you of the sad situation in my country today and of the aspirations of my people, because in our struggle for freedom, truth is the only weapon we possess."

—*THE DALAI LAMA* (1989)

"Buddhism, the foundation of traditional Burmese culture, places the greatest value on man, who alone of all beings can achieve the supreme state of Buddhahood. Each man has in him the potential to realize the truth through his own will and endeavor and to help others to realize it. Human life therefore is infinitely precious."

—*AUNG SAN SUU KYI* (1991)

"I consider this Prize, not as an award to me personally, but rather as one of the greatest conquests in the struggle for peace, for Human Rights and for the rights of the indigenous people who, for 500 years, have been split, fragmented, as well as the victims of genocides, repression and discrimination."

—*RIGOBERTA MENCHU TUM* (1992)

"The historical development in Guatemala reflects now the need and the irreversibility of the active contribution of women to the configuration of the new Guatemalan social order, of which, I humbly believe, the Indian women already are a clear testimony. This Nobel Peace Prize is a recognition to those who have been, and still are in most parts of the world, the most exploited of the exploited; the most discriminated of the discriminated; the most marginalized of the marginalized, but still those who produce life and riches."

—*RIGOBERTA MENCHU TUM* *(1992)*

"As a member of a people, I have to share the destiny of the people, taking upon myself completely this mandate, knowing the risks that such attitude will involve. Striving for the defense of the rights of all peoples is not only the privilege of those guiding the destiny of the people or those enjoying lofty positions in society, but it is the duty of everyone whatever rank or status."

—*CARLOS FILIPE XIMENES BELO* *(1996)*

"I do believe for sure that among us we have something in common, that is we affirm that the human being is the subject of all concept and human activities. We declare that one's value and dignity does not depend on the individual's belief, religion, politics, philosophy, race, or color of skin. Man is a being realized when there is a reciprocity of respect. It means that wherever human beings are not respected in their elementary rights by those in charge or by those responsible in society, as a consequence, we have oppression, slavery, arrogance, arbitrariness, death of individuals, and death of a people."

—*CARLOS FILIPE XIMENES BELO* *(1996)*

"Let us always think of many anonymous people throughout the world, struggling for the protection of human rights. Day by day, working to convince the international community of the justice of their cause, whether they be Moslems or Christians, Protestants or Catholics, Hindus or Buddhists whether they be followers of age-old traditional beliefs, believers or non-believers. I say: press on, take courage, remain true to your ideals, you will not be forgotten."

—*CARLOS FILIPE XIMENES BELO* (1996)

"From the Chittagon Hill Tracts in Bangladesh to Bougainville, Kurdistan, Sri Lanka, India, Tibet, Chechnya, Ogoni, West Papua, millions of peoples seek to assert their most fundamental rights and if we attempt to find a common denominator for the problems I have just listed there is one: the right of peoples to self-determination."

—*JOSÉ RAMOS-HORTA* (1996)

"We believe that human rights transcend boundaries and must prevail over state sovereignty."

—*JOSÉ RAMOS-HORTA* (1996)

"The basis of peace and stability, in any society, has to be the fullest respect for the human rights of all its people."

—*JOHN HUME* (1998)

"Bringing medical aid to people in distress is an attempt to defend them against what is aggressive to them as human beings. Humanitarian action is more than simple generosity, simple charity. It aims to build spaces of normalcy in the midst of what is profoundly abnormal. More than offering material assistance, we aim to enable individuals to regain their rights and dignity as human beings. As an independent volunteer association, we are committed to bringing direct medical aid to people in need. But we act not in a vacuum, and we speak not into the wind, but with a clear intent to assist, to provoke change, or to reveal injustice. Our action and our voice is an act of indignation, a refusal to accept an active or passive assault on the other."

—*JAMES ORBINSKI,* representing Médecins
Sans Frontières *(1999)*

"The knowledge and information age of the 21st century promises to be an age of enormous wealth. But it also presents the danger of hugely growing wealth gaps between and within countries. The problem presents itself as a serious threat to human rights and peace. In the new century, we must continue the fight against the forces that suppress democracy and resort to violence. We must also strive to deal with the new challenge to human rights and peace with steps to alleviate the information gap, to help the developing countries and the marginalized sectors of society to catch up with the new age."

—*KIM DAE-JUNG (2000)*

"Today's real borders are not between nations, but between powerful and powerless, free and fettered, privileged and humiliated. Today, no walls can separate humanitarian or human rights crises in one part of the world from national security crises in another."

—*KOFI ANNAN (2001)*

"In the introduction to my speech, I spoke of human rights as a guarantor of freedom, justice, and peace. If human rights fail to be manifested in codified laws or put into effect by states, then, as rendered in the preamble of the Universal Declaration of Human Rights, human beings will be left with no choice other than staging a 'rebellion against tyranny and oppression.' A human being divested of all dignity, a human being deprived of human rights, a human being gripped by starvation, a human being beaten by famine, war, and illness, a humiliated human being and a plundered human being is not in any position or state to recover the rights he or she has lost.

"If the 21st century wishes to free itself from the cycle of violence, acts of terror and war, and avoid repetition of the experience of the 20th century–that most disaster-ridden century of humankind—there is no other way except by understanding and putting into practice every human right for all mankind, irrespective of race, gender, faith, nationality, or social status."

—*SHIRIN EBADI (2003)*

"So, together, we have planted over 30 million trees that provide fuel, food, shelter, and income to support their children's education and household needs. The activity also creates employment and improves soils and watersheds. Through their involvement, women gain some degree of power over their lives, especially their social and economic position and relevance in the family. This work continues.

"Initially, the work was difficult because historically our people have been persuaded to believe that because they are poor, they lack not only capital, but also knowledge and skills to address their challenges. Instead they are conditioned to believe that solutions to their problems must come from 'outside.' Further, women did not realize that meeting their needs depended on their environment being healthy and well managed. They were also unaware that a degraded environment leads to a scramble for scarce resources and may culminate in poverty and even conflict. They were also unaware of the injustices of international economic arrangements."

—WANGARI MAATHAI (2004)

"We are 1,000 people here today in this august hall. Imagine for a moment that we represent the world's population. These 200 people on my left would be the wealthy of the world, who consume 80 percent of the available resources. And these 400 people on my right would be living on an income of less than $2 per day.

"This underprivileged group of people on my right is no less intelligent or less worthy than their fellow human beings on the other side of the aisle. They were simply born into this fate.

"In the real world, this imbalance in living conditions inevitably leads to inequality of opportunity, and in many cases loss of hope. And what is worse, all too often the plight of the poor is compounded by and results in human rights abuses, a lack of good governance, and a deep sense of injustice. This combination naturally creates a most fertile breeding ground for civil wars, organized crime, and extremism in its different forms."

—MOHAMED ELBARADEI (2005)

"Peace should be understood in a human way—in a broad social, political, and economic way. Peace is threatened by unjust economic, social, and political order, absence of democracy, environmental degradation, and absence of human rights.

"Poverty is the absence of all human rights. The frustrations, hostility, and anger generated by abject poverty cannot sustain peace in any society. For building stable peace we must find ways to provide opportunities for people to live decent lives."

—MUHAMMAD YUNUS (2006)

Archbishop Desmond Tutu preaching in Hartford, Connecticut, on his tour of the United States (1986).

POLITICS
AND
LEADERSHIP

"The grim fact, however, is that we prepare for war like precocious giants and for peace like retarded pygmies."

—*LESTER B. PEARSON* (1957)

"Nansen was the first to say what others have repeated, that 'the difficult is what takes a little while; the impossible is what takes a little longer.' If politics is the art of the possible, statesmanship is the art, in Nansen's sense, of the impossible; and it is statesmanship that our perplexed and tortured humanity requires today."

—*PHILIP NOEL-BAKER* (1959)

"I do not feel like making loud appeals, for it is easy to demand moderation, reason and modesty of others. But this plea comes from the bottom of my heart: May all those who possess the power to wage war have the mastery of reason to maintain peace."

—*WILLY BRANDT* (1971)

"I pay no attention to those doubters and detractors unwilling to believe that a lasting peace can be genuinely embraced by those who march under a different ideological banner or those who are more accustomed to cannons of war than to councils of peace.

"We seek in Central America not peace alone, not peace to be followed someday by political progress, but peace and democracy, together, indivisible, an end to the shedding of human blood, which is inseparable from an end to the suppression of human rights. We do not judge, much less condemn, any other nation's political or ideological system, freely chosen and never exported. We cannot require sovereign states to conform to patterns of government not of their own choosing. But we can and do insist that every government respect those universal rights of man that have meaning beyond national boundaries and ideological labels. We believe that justice and peace can only thrive together, never apart. A nation that mistreats its own citizens is more likely to mistreat its neighbors."

—*OSCAR ARIAS SÁNCHEZ (1987)*

"I come from a world with huge problems, which we shall overcome in freedom. I come from a world in a hurry, because hunger cannot wait. When hope is forgotten, violence does not delay. Dogmatism is too impatient for dialogue. . . . I come from a world which cannot wait for the guerrilla and the soldier to hold their fire: young people are dying, brothers are dying, and tomorrow who can tell why. I come from a world which cannot wait to open prison gates not, as before, for free men to go in, but for those imprisoned to come out.

"America's liberty and democracy have no time to lose, and we need the whole world's understanding to win freedom from dictators, to win freedom from misery.

"I come from Central America.

"I accept this prize as one of 27 million Central Americans. Behind the democratic awakening in Central America lies over a century of merciless dictatorships and general injustice and poverty. The choice before my little America is whether to suffer another century of violence, or to achieve peace by overcoming the fear of liberty. Only peace can write the new history."

—*OSCAR ARIAS SÁNCHEZ* (*1987*)

"History can only move towards liberty. History can only have justice at its heart. To march in the opposite direction to history is to be on the road to shame, poverty and oppression. Without freedom, there is no revolution. All oppression runs counter to man's spirit."

—*OSCAR ARIAS SÁNCHEZ* (*1987*)

"Knowledge and trust are the foundations of a new world order. Hence the necessity, in my view, to learn to forecast the course of events in various regions of the globe, by pooling the efforts of scientists, philosophers and humanitarian thinkers within the UN framework. Policies, even the most prudent and precise, are made by man. We need maximum insurance to guarantee that decisions taken by members of the world community should not affect the security, sovereignty and vital interests of its other members or damage the natural environment and the moral climate of the world.

"I am an optimist and I believe that together we shall be able now to make the right historical choice so as not to miss the great chance at the turn of centuries and millennia and make the current extremely difficult transition to a peaceful world order. A balance of interests rather than a balance of power, a search for compromise and concord rather than a search for advantages at other people's expense, and respect for equality rather than claims to leadership—such are the elements which can provide the groundwork for world progress and which should be readily acceptable for reasonable people informed by the experience of the 20th century."

—*MIKHAIL GORBACHEV* *(1990)*

"Countries used to divide the world into their friends and foes. No longer. The foes now are universal—poverty, famine, religious radicalization, desertification, drugs, proliferation of nuclear weapons, ecological devastation. They threaten all nations, just as science and information are the potential friends of all nations.

"Classical diplomacy and strategy were aimed at identifying enemies and confronting them. Now they have to identify dangers, global or local, and tackle them before they become disasters."

—*SHIMON PERES* *(1994)*

"Science must be learned; it cannot be conquered. An army that can occupy knowledge has yet to be built. And that is why armies of occupation are a thing of the past. Indeed, even for defensive purposes, a country cannot rely on its army alone. Territorial frontiers are no obstacle to ballistic missiles, and no weapon can shield from a nuclear device. Today, therefore, the battle for survival must be based on political wisdom and moral vision no less than on military might."

—*SHIMON PERES* *(1994)*

"The preservation of the territorial integrity of a country can be achieved only if those in power are sensitive to the basic demands and aspirations of the many indigenous peoples and

121

nationalities that make up the country. Brute force might silence and keep dormant the dreams and aspirations of a people but the anger simmering for decades will inevitably resurface and break up the country."

—*JOSÉ RAMOS-HORTA (1996)*

"Sometimes in history individuals in power are driven to commit wanton crimes but those who survive and are in power today should resist the temptation to exact revenge in the name of justice. In victory be magnanimous."

—*JOSÉ RAMOS-HORTA (1996)*

"It is recognition of the fact that NGOs have worked in close cooperation with governments for the first time on an arms control issue, with the United Nations, with the International Committee of the Red Cross. Together, we have set a precedent. Together, we have changed history. The closing remarks of the French ambassador in Oslo to me were the best. She said, 'This is historic not just because of the treaty. This is historic because, for the first time, the leaders of states have come together to answer the will of civil society.'"

—*JODY WILLIAMS (1997)*

"Too many lives have already been lost in Ireland in the pursuit of political goals. Bloodshed for political change prevents the only change that truly matters—in the human heart. We must now shape a future of change that will be truly radical and that will offer a focus for real unity of purpose—

harnessing new forces of idealism and commitment for the benefit of Ireland and all its people."

—*JOHN HUME* *(1998)*

"I am personally and perhaps culturally conditioned to be sceptical of speeches which are full of sound and fury, idealistic in intention, but impossible of implementation; and I resist the kind of rhetoric which substitutes vapor for vision. Instinctively, I identify with the person who said that when he heard a politician talk of his vision, he recommended him to consult an optician! But, if you want to hear of a possible Northern Ireland, not a utopia, but a normal and decent society, flawed as human beings are flawed, but fair as human beings are fair, then I hope not to disappoint you."

—*DAVID TRIMBLE* *(1998)*

"The realization of peace needs more than magnanimity. It requires a certain political prudence, and a willingness at times not to be too precise or pedantic. The eighteenth-century political philosopher Edmund Burke says, 'It is the nature of greatness not to be exact.' Distinguished Israeli writer Amos Oz agrees, 'Inconsistency is the basis of coexistence. The heroes of tragedy driven by consistency and by righteousness, destroy each other. He who seeks total supreme justice seeks death.'"

—*DAVID TRIMBLE* *(1998)*

"Some critics complain that I lack 'the vision thing.' But vision in its pure meaning is clear sight. That does not mean I have no dreams. I do. But I try to have them at night. By day I am satisfied if I can see the furthest limit of what is possible. Politics can be likened to driving at night over unfamiliar hills and mountains. Close attention must be paid to what the beam can reach and the next bend. Driving by day, as I believe we are now doing, we should drive steadily, not recklessly, studying the countryside ahead, with judicious glances in the mirror. We should be encouraged by having come so far, and face into the next hill, rather than the mountain beyond. It is not that the mountain is not in my mind, but the hill has to be climbed first. There are hills in Northern Ireland and there are mountains. The hills are decommissioning and policing. But the mountain, if we could but see it clearly, is not in front of us but behind us, in history. The dark shadow we seem to see in the distance is not really a mountain ahead, but the shadow of the mountain behind—a shadow from the past thrown forward into our future. It is a dark sludge of historical sectarianism. We can leave it behind us if we wish."

—*DAVID TRIMBLE (1998)*

"Politics is the bedrock to which all societies return. Because we are the only agents of change who accept man as he is and not as someone else wants him to be. The work we do may be grubby and without glamour. But it has one saving grace. It is grounded on reality and reason. What is the nature of that reason? Let [Edmund] Burke answer, 'Political reason is computing principle: adding, subtracting, multiplying, and dividing, morally—and not metaphysically or mathematically—true moral denominations.'"

—*DAVID TRIMBLE (1998)*

"In Ulster, what I have looked for is a peace within the realms of the possible. We could only have started from where we actually were, not from where we would have liked to be. And we have started. And we will go on. And we will go on all the better if we walk, rather than run. If we put aside fantasy and accept the flawed nature of human enterprises. Sometimes we will stumble, maybe even go back a bit. But this need not matter if in the spirit of an old Irish proverb we say to ourselves, 'Tomorrow is another day.'"

—*DAVID TRIMBLE*   *(1998)*

"In the decades of my struggle for democracy, I was constantly faced with the refutation that western-style democracy was not suitable for Asia, that Asia lacked the roots. This is far from true. In Asia, long before the west, the respect for human dignity was written into systems of thought, and intellectual traditions upholding the concept of 'demos' took root. 'The people are heaven. The will of the people is the will of heaven. Revere the people, as you would heaven.' This was the central tenet in the political thoughts of China and Korea as early as three thousand years ago."

—*KIM DAE-JUNG*   *(2000)*

"We thus inherit from the 20th century the political as well as the scientific and technological power, which—if only we have the will to use them—give us the chance to vanquish poverty, ignorance, and disease.

"In the 21st century I believe the mission of the United Nations will be defined by a new, more profound awareness of the sanctity and dignity of every human life, regardless of race

125

or religion. This will require us to look beyond the framework of states, and beneath the surface of nations or communities. We must focus, as never before, on improving the conditions of the individual men and women who give the state or nation its richness and character. We must begin with the young Afghan girl, recognizing that saving that one life is to save humanity itself."

—*KOFI ANNAN (2001)*

"From this vision of the role of the United Nations in the next century flow three key priorities for the future: eradicating poverty, preventing conflict, and promoting democracy. Only in a world that is rid of poverty can all men and women make the most of their abilities. Only where individual rights are respected can differences be channeled politically and resolved peacefully. Only in a democratic environment, based on respect for diversity and dialogue, can individual self-expression and self-government be secured, and freedom of association be upheld."

—*KOFI ANNAN (2001)*

"There is also need to galvanize civil society and grassroots movements to catalyze change. I call upon governments to recognize the role of these social movements in building a critical mass of responsible citizens, who help maintain checks and balances in society. On their part, civil society should embrace not only their rights but also their responsibilities."

—*WANGARI MAATHAI (2004)*

"Consider our development aid record. Last year, the nations of the world spent over $1 trillion on armaments. But we contributed less than 10 percent of that amount—a mere $80 billion—as official development assistance to the developing parts of the world, where 850 million people suffer from hunger.

"My friend James Morris heads the World Food Program, whose task it is to feed the hungry. He recently told me, 'If I could have just 1 percent of the money spent on global armaments, no one in this world would go to bed hungry.'"

—*MOHAMED ELBARADEI (2005)*

"Imagine what would happen if the nations of the world spent as much on development as on building the machines of war. Imagine a world where every human being would live in freedom and dignity. Imagine a world in which we would shed the same tears when a child dies in Darfur or Vancouver. Imagine a world where we would settle our differences through diplomacy and dialogue and not through bombs or bullets. Imagine if the only nuclear weapons remaining were the relics in our museums. Imagine the legacy we could leave to our children.

"Imagine that such a world is within our grasp."

—*MOHAMED ELBARADEI (2005)*

"I believe terrorism cannot be won over by military action. Terrorism must be condemned in the strongest language. We must stand solidly against it, and find all the means to end it. We must address the root causes of terrorism to end it for all time to come. I believe that putting resources into improving the lives of the poor people is a better strategy than spending it on guns."

—*MUHAMMAD YUNUS (2006)*

127

"I support globalization and believe it can bring more benefits to the poor than its alternative. But it must be the right kind of globalization. To me, globalization is like a hundred-lane highway criss-crossing the world. If it is a free-for-all highway, its lanes will be taken over by the giant trucks from powerful economies. Bangladeshi rickshaw will be thrown off the highway. In order to have a win-win globalization we must have traffic rules, traffic police, and traffic authority for this global highway. Rule of 'strongest takes it all' must be replaced by rules that ensure that the poorest have a place and piece of the action, without being elbowed out by the strong. Globalization must not become financial imperialism."

—*Muhammad Yunus (2006)*

"We get what we want, or what we don't refuse. We accept the fact that we will always have poor people around us, and that poverty is part of human destiny. This is precisely why we continue to have poor people around us. If we firmly believe that poverty is unacceptable to us, and that it should not belong to a civilized society, we would have built appropriate institutions and policies to create a poverty-free world.

"We wanted to go to the moon, so we went there. We achieve what we want to achieve. If we are not achieving something, it is because we have not put our minds to it. We create what we want.

"What we want and how we get to it depends on our mindsets. It is extremely difficult to change mindsets once they are formed. We create the world in accordance with our mindset. We need to invent ways to change our perspective continually and reconfigure our mindset quickly as new knowledge emerges. We can reconfigure our world if we can reconfigure our mindset."

—*MUHAMMAD YUNUS (2006)*

"I firmly believe that we can create a poverty-free world if we collectively believe in it. In a poverty-free world, the only place you would be able to see poverty is in the poverty museums. When school children take a tour of the poverty museums, they would be horrified to see the misery and indignity that some human beings had to go through. They would blame their forefathers for tolerating this inhuman condition, which existed for so long, for so many people."

—*MUHAMMAD YUNUS (2006)*

"The future is knocking at our door right now. Make no mistake, the next generation will ask us one of two questions. Either they will ask: 'What were you thinking; why didn't you act?'

"Or they will ask instead: 'How did you find the moral courage to rise and successfully resolve a crisis that so many said was impossible to solve?'

"We have everything we need to get started, save perhaps political will, but political will is a renewable resource.

"So let us renew it, and say together: 'We have a purpose. We are many. For this purpose we will rise, and we will act.'"

—*AL GORE, JR. (2007)*

BIOGRAPHICAL NOTES

The following biographical entries include only those prize winners whose speeches and lectures have been excerpted for this volume. For a listing of all of the prize winners, the reader may refer to the Chronology on pages 139–140.

Note: The italicized date in each entry represents the year for which the prize was awarded; on several occasions the Nobel Committee postponed its decision for a certain year and then made the grant of that year's prize one year later.

AMERICAN FRIENDS SERVICE COMMITTEE of the United States and the **FRIENDS SERVICE COUNCIL** of Great Britain. *1947.* HENRY J. CADBURY and MARGARET BACKHOUSE, respectively, represented these Quaker organizations, awarded the Nobel Peace Prize for their relief and reconstruction work during and after World War II.

AMNESTY INTERNATIONAL (1961–). *1977.* This international organization that defends the rights of prisoners of conscience was represented at the award ceremony by its chairman, THOMAS HAMMARBERG of Sweden, who gave the acceptance speech, and its vice-chairman, MÜMTAZ SOYSAL of Turkey, who delivered the lecture.

ANGELL, NORMAN (1872–1967). *1933.* British author of the noted peace book *The Great Illusion,* who served the cause for many years as a very influential publicist and lecturer.

ANNAN, KOFI. See United Nations.

ARAFAT, YASSER (1929–2004). *1994.* Chairman of the Palestine Liberation Organization, who shared the prize with Prime Minister YITZHAK RABIN and Foreign Minister SHIMON PERES of Israel for "their efforts to create peace in the Middle East." Born in Cairo to a Palestinian family, Arafat lived briefly in Jerusalem, but he has spent most of his life in exile from Palestine, fighting in many ways, including by arms and terrorism, for freedom and independence for his people. When he renounced terrorism and recognized Israel's right to exist, secret negotiations could begin which led to the agreement of 1993 to end the long bitter conflict. Arafat could then return to the Gaza Strip of Palestine as President of the Palestinian National Authority. Further implementation of the agreement is the subject of continuing negotiations.

ARIAS SÁNCHEZ, OSCAR (1941–   ). *1987.* President of Costa Rica, a democratic country without an army, who succeeded in gaining the approval of the four other presidents of the region for his peace plan for Central America. The Nobel Committee hoped that its prize would aid his efforts. After he left the Presidency, he remained active working for international peace.

ARNOLDSON, KLAUS PONTUS (1844–1916). *1908.* Sweden's leading peace activist. Inspired by his liberal Christianity, he served the peace cause as a politician, organizer, and influential orator and publicist.

AUNG SAN SUU KYI [pronounced "Sue Chee"] (1945–   ). *1991.* The daughter of General Aung San, founder of Burma's independence, she returned from abroad in 1988 to lead the democracy movement against the military dictatorship. The government placed her under house arrest and ignored the results of the national election, which her party won decisively. She was kept in detention for six years until July 1995, but she has remained the center of widespread aspirations for freedom and democracy in her country (now called Myanmar). The Nobel Committee gave her the prize for her "nonviolent struggle for democracy and human rights," calling this "one of the most extraordinary examples of civil courage in Asia in recent decades." Her son Alexander, in his speech accepting the prize in her behalf, quoted the passages from her *Freedom from Fear* which are reprinted in this volume (with the kind permission of Penguin Books). Although she is no longer under house arrest, her movements are still restricted.

BACKHOUSE, MARGARET. See American Friends Service Committee of the United States.

BALCH, EMILY GREENE (1867–1961). *1946.* Scholar and intellectual leader of the American peace movement. With Jane Addams (Peace Prize winner, 1931) she was a co-founder of the Women's International League for Peace and Freedom, for which she worked many years in Geneva and in the United States.

BEGIN, MENACHEM (1913–1992), and **MOHAMMED ANWAR EL-SADAT** (1918–1981). *1978.* Prime Minister of Israel and President of the Arab Republic of Egypt, respectively, they were given the prize for their agreement at Camp David, where they had been brought together by President Jimmy Carter, to end the state of war between their two countries that had lasted for thirty years. Sadat's peace policy was criticized by many Egyptians and by other Arab states, and he decided not to appear with Begin at Oslo but to send his counselor Sayed Marei to read his speech of acceptance. The award ceremony was moved to the Akershus fortress to provide more security for Begin when he delivered his own acceptance speech.

BELO, CARLOS FILIPE XIMENES (1948–). *1996.* Born on the tropical island of Timor, in 1988, he was consecrated as bishop. He was a vocal advocate for the human rights of the people of East Timor. His work led to several proclamations issued by the United Nations that criticized Indonesia and embarrassed its leaders. He was awarded the Nobel Peace Prize for his dedicated defense of the human rights of the East Timorese.

BORLAUG, NORMAN (1914–). *1970.* American agricultural scientist whose impact on the increased production of wheat, maize, and rice earned him the title "father of the Green Revolution." In the words of the Nobel Committee: "More than any other single person in this age, he has helped to provide bread for a hungry world. We have made this choice in the hope that providing bread will also give the world peace."

BOURGEOIS, LÉON (1851–1925). *1920.* French political leader who helped prepare the way for the establishment of the League of Nations, both in his writings and throughout his political career. He chaired the French delegation at both intergovernmental peace conferences at The Hague and helped write the Covenant of the League at the Paris Peace Conference. Ill and unable to attend the award ceremony, Bourgeois sent a "Communication" to the Nobel Committee in December 1922, from which these excerpts are taken.

BOYD-ORR OF BRECHIN, LORD (1880–1971). *1949.*
John Boyd-Orr was a Scottish medical doctor and nutritionist,
a founder and director general of the United Nations Food and
Agricultural Organization and later a prominent international
peace leader.

BRANDT, WILLY (1913–1992). *1971.* The second German
statesman to be honored for his policy of peace and reconciliation with former enemy states. As foreign minister and chan-
cellor of the Federal Republic, Brandt strengthened ties with
Western European states and negotiated peace pacts with
Poland and the Soviet Union. After leaving office, he continued to work for peace as a leader of the world's Social
Democrats.

BUNCHE, RALPH J. (1904–1971). *1950.* American social
scientist who served as a State Department official and then as
a top UN administrator. As UN mediator, he negotiated the
ending of the Arab-Jewish hostilities over Palestine in 1949.

CADBURY, HENRY J. See American Friends Service
Committee of the United States.

CARTER, JIMMY (1924–). *2002.* Thirty-ninth president
of the United States of America (1977-81), whose term was
highlighted by the signing of the Panama Canal treaties, the
Camp David Accords, the Egypt-Israel peace treaty, and the
Strategic Arms Limitation Treaty (SALT) II treaty with the
Soviet Union. After his presidency he founded the Carter
Center, dedicated to protecting human rights and well-
regarded for its international election monitoring programs

and its efforts to eliminate sickness and poverty throughout the world.

CHAPUISAT, ÉDOUARD. See International Committee of the Red Cross.

CHAZOV, DR. EVGENY. See International Physicians for the Prevention of Nuclear War.

DAE-JUNG, KIM (1925–). *2000.* Fifteenth president of the Republic of Korea (1998-2003). Born in a small island village off the coast of South Korea, he entered politics in response to the increasingly dictatorial nature of the government. In the course of his political career, Dae-jung endured a military coup d'état, election rigging, jail time, exile, house arrest, a kidnapping, a death sentence, and five assassination attempts. His first acts in office were to revive the country from economic collapse and to reach out to North Korea. Dae-jung was awarded the Nobel Peace Prize for his efforts to reunify North and South Korea.

DALAI LAMA XIV of Tibet, **TENZIN GYATSO** (1935–). *1989.* Enthroned in 1940 as the spiritual and temporal ruler of Tibet, he went into exile in India in 1959, after the Chinese, who regard Tibet as part of China, sent in their army to establish control. Since then he has worked untiringly from abroad to liberate his people. He was given the prize for this championing of human rights by the means of nonviolence, for his Buddhist message of love and compassion, and for his efforts to awaken concern for the environment.

EBADI, SHIRIN (1947–). *2003*. An Iranian lawyer, human rights activist, and founder of Children's Rights Support Association in Iran, Ebadi became the first woman judge to preside over a legislative court in Iran in 1975. Following the Islamic Revolution in 1979, she was removed from that position. Upon obtaining a lawyer's license in 1992, she set up her own legal practice, handling many high-profile cases. She received the Nobel Peace Prize for her work as a champion of human rights, especially for women and children.

ELBARADEI, MOHAMED. See the International Atomic Energy Agency.

FRIENDS SERVICE COUNCIL of Great Britain. See American Friends Service Committee of the United States.

GORBACHEV, MIKHAIL SERGEYEVICH (1931–). *1990*. Born to a peasant family, he won admission to law school and worked his way up through the ranks of the Communist Party to become at the age of 54 the party general secretary and head of the government of the Soviet Union. With his policies of *perestroika* (restructuring) and *glasnost* (openness), he began major economic and political reforms which liberated the life and thought of the country from the stagnation of the party dictatorship. In 1989 he became president of the Soviet Union. His foreign policies brought about the end of the Cold War, the achievement which won him the prize. He sent a message of acceptance to be read at the award ceremony, but he was unable to deliver his Nobel lecture in Oslo until June 1991. This occasion marked the high point of his international acclaim. At home, economic difficulties made him very unpopular. In August an attempted coup by hard-liners was thwarted, but Gorbachev's position was badly weakened and the power of the central government over the Soviet republics severely diminished. By December the Soviet Union had disintegrated, and Gorbachev, now president with no country over which to preside, formally resigned his office.

GORE, AL, JR. (1948–   ). *2007.* Forty-fifth vice president of the United States (1993-2001), under President Bill Clinton. Gore previously served in the U.S. House of Representatives (1977–85) and the U.S. Senate (1985–93). A prominent environmental activist, he shared the 2007 Nobel Peace Prize with the INTERGOVERNMENTAL PANEL ON CLIMATE CHANGE "for their efforts to build up and disseminate greater knowledge about man-made climate change, and to lay the foundations for the measures that are needed to counteract such change." In 2006, he starred in the Academy Award–winning documentary film *An Inconvenient Truth* about global warming.

GRAMEEN BANK. See Yunus, Muhammad.

HARTLING, POUL. See Office of the United Nations High Commissioner for Refugees.

HENDERSON, ARTHUR (1863–1935). *1934.* British foreign secretary known for his peace policies and his strong support of the League of Nations. As president of the World Disarmament Conference (1932–1935), he worked valiantly but in vain to make it a success.

HOLDREN, JOHN P. See Pugwash Conferences on Science and World Affairs.

HUME, JOHN. (1937–). *1998.* An enduring figure on Northern Ireland's political stage, John Hume spent decades working toward a resolution of the province's sectarian conflict. As leader of the Social Democratic and Labour Party (SDLP), the main moderate nationalist party of Northern Ireland's Catholic minority, he steadfastly denounced the violent tactics of the paramilitary Irish Republican Army (IRA) and pursued closer ties with the overwhelmingly Catholic Republic of Ireland through peaceful means only. His efforts to bring Sinn Fein, a Catholic party with ties to the IRA, into peace negotiations made him instrumental in forging a landmark all-party accord in 1998.

INTERGOVERNMENTAL PANEL ON CLIMATE CHANGE (1988–). *2007.* A scientific intergovernmental body set up by the World Meteorological Organization and by the United Nations Environment Programme to evaluate the risk of climate change caused by human activity. The prize was accepted by R. K. PACHAURI, Chairman of the IPCC, and shared with AL GORE, JR.

INTERNATIONAL ATOMIC ENERGY AGENCY (1957–). *2005.* The prize was jointly awarded to the IAEA, an intergovernmental organization under the auspices of the United Nations, and its Director General MOHAMED EL-BARADEI (1947–), an Egyptian diplomat, for their work in promoting the safe and peaceful use of nuclear power and their efforts in preventing the militarization of nuclear weapons.

INTERNATIONAL CAMPAIGN TO BAN LAND-MINES. *1997.* A grassroots movement, now representing 1,400 nongovernmental organizations, that in the course of a few years worked with governments to change a ban on anti-personnel mines from a vision to a feasible reality: the Mine Ban Treaty of 1997. RAE MCGRATH is founder of Mines Advisory Group, a founding member organization of the ICBL.

INTERNATIONAL COMMITTEE OF THE RED CROSS. *1944.* At the award ceremony held in December 1945 MAX HUBER, honorary president, accepted the prize in behalf of the ICRC, the second of the three which this Swiss organization has received. The first was awarded in 1917. ÉDOUARD CHAPUISAT, a member of the ICRC, gave the Nobel lecture. See The League of Red Cross Societies for the 1963 award.

INTERNATIONAL PHYSICIANS FOR THE PREVEN-TION OF NUCLEAR WAR (IPPNW) (1980–). *1985.* DR. EVGENY CHAZOV of the Soviet Union and DR. BERNARD LOWN of the United States were invited by the Nobel Committee to receive the prize as co-presidents of IPPNW, an international federation with members in forty countries. The Nobel Committee had been impressed both with the message of IPPNW that there could be no adequate medical response to nuclear warfare and with the cooperation of Soviet and American physicians.

KING, MARTIN LUTHER, JR. (1929–1968). *1964.* The leader of the nonviolent movement for civil rights in the United States. A Baptist minister who had undertaken advanced studies, his sermons and speeches are considered among the best examples of American oratory. The chairman of the Norwegian Nobel Committee declared: "He is the first person in the Western world to have shown us that a struggle can be waged without violence. He is the first to make the message of brotherly love a reality in the course of his struggle, and he has brought this message to all men, to all nations and races."

de KLERK, FREDERIK WILLEM (1936–   ). *1993.* Son of a leading politician of South Africa, he graduated in law and became a prominent member of the ruling National Party. After holding a number of ministerial posts, in 1989 he became the leader of the party and then state president. In 1990 he freed NELSON MANDELA from prison and, courageously reversing the policies of his party, dismantled apartheid and worked with Mandela to prepare the way for free non-racist elections. For their cooperation in peacefully ending the racial conflict and laying the foundation for a new democratic country, they received the prize. As a result of the elections, de Klerk became a vice-president of South Africa. He later withdrew from political life.

LANGE, CHRISTIAN L. (1869–1938). *1921.* A leading Norwegian internationalist, both as a scholar and as the longtime secretary-general of the Interparliamentary Union and a member of the Norwegian delegation to the Assembly of the League of Nations.

THE LEAGUE OF RED CROSS SOCIETIES. *1963.* In this centenary year of the founding of the Red Cross, the League shared the prize with the **INTERNATIONAL COMMITTEE OF THE RED CROSS.** JOHN A. MACAULAY, the Canadian jurist who was chairman of the board of governors of the League in Geneva, delivered the Nobel lecture in its behalf.

LOWN, DR. BERNARD. See International Physicians for the Prevention of Nuclear War.

LUTULI, ALBERT JOHN (1898–1967). *1960.* Zulu tribal chief in South Africa, president of the African National Congress, and leader in the nonviolent struggle against the policies of apartheid.

MAATHAI, WANGARI (1940–). *2004.* An environmental and political activist from Kenya, Maathai became the first African woman to receive the Nobel Peace Prize for "her contribution to sustainable development, democracy, and peace." Dr. Maathai was elected to the Parliament of Kenya in 2002, and served as Assistant Minister for Environment and Natural Resources (2003-05). Through her Green Belt Movement, a grassroots environmental nongovernmental organization of women's groups, founded in 1977, Maathai has been instrumental in the planting of more than 30 million trees across Kenya to prevent soil erosion.

MACAULAY, JOHN A. See The League of Red Cross Societies.

MacBRIDE, SEAN (1904–1988). *1974.* Once an Irish revolutionary and always a passionate nationalist, MacBride became a strong internationalist who was honored with the Peace Prize for his championship of human rights. As Irish foreign minister, he gained the approval of the Council of Europe for the European Convention on Human Rights. He helped found Amnesty International (1961, Peace Prize in 1977), as a lawyer promoted human rights through the International Commission of Jurists, and held top positions in various international peace organizations.

MANDELA, NELSON ROHIHLAHIA (1918–   ). *1993.* Mandela was president of the African National Congress (ANC) when he shared the prize with President FREDERICK W. de KLERK of the Republic of South Africa. In 1990 de Klerk had freed him from prison, where Mandela had been incarcerated for almost 28 years for his activities opposing apartheid and where he had become the most celebrated prisoner of the time and the symbol of the struggle in South Africa for racial justice. He emerged from prison to assume the leadership of the ANC and, unembittered and in the spirit of reconciliation, to cooperate with de Klerk to end apartheid and to arrange for free all-race elections. For thus ending the conflict peacefully, the two were granted the prize. The elections, held in 1994, resulted in Mandela's replacing de Klerk as state president. He served until 1999.

MARSHALL, GEORGE C. (1880–1959). *1953.* General Marshall served the United States for many years as an army officer, finally as chief of staff during World War II, making a most important contribution to the victory. He served also as secretary of state and of defense. In the former position his

"Marshall Plan" of economic assistance brought about the re-construction of Europe's economy after the war. For this he was awarded the Peace Prize.

McGRATH, RAE. See International Campaign to Ban Landmines.

MÉDECINS SANS FRONTIÈRES (DOCTORS WITHOUT BORDERS). *1999.* Since its foundation in 1971, Médecins Sans Frontières, headquartered in Brussels, Belgium, has adhered to the fundamental principle that all disaster victims, whether the disaster is natural or human in origin, have a right to professional assistance, given as quickly and efficiently as possible. Unlike most humanitarian organi-zations, MSF protests publicly when the human rights of the peoples they help are violated. JAMES ORBINSKI is the or-ganization's president.

MENCHU TUM, RIGOBERTA (1959–   ). *1992.* Born to a poor Indian peasant family in Guatemala, she knew well the hardy toil and brutal oppression that were her people's lot. From the Catholic church she gained a scanty education, while her mother taught her the ways of Mayan culture. The army used methods of great cruelty to keep the Indians from joining the anti-government guerrillas, and her brother, her father and her mother were all tortured and killed by soldiers. She decided, however, to work peacefully for social justice, and in her early twenties she was taking leadership in strikes and demonstrations. She had to go into hiding and then flee abroad, where she gained for the cause of the Indian peasants an international hearing, having taught herself Spanish to interpret her message. For her indefatigable work for the rights of indigenous peoples and for "ethnocultural reconciliation" she was awarded the Peace Prize. As she explained, "Peace is not a little white dove. It is you and me."

MONETA, ERNESTO TEODORO (1830–1918). *1907.* Journalist and editor who headed the Italian peace movement. In his youth Moneta had taken part in the struggle for unification of his country, and he hoped for a peace based upon fraternal relationships between peoples who had achieved their freedom and national unity.

MYRDAL, ALVA REIMER (1902–1986). *1982.* Swedish social reformer, cabinet minister, and diplomat, co-winner with **ALFONSO GARCÍA ROBLES,** former Mexican foreign minister, for their efforts to promote disarmament. Both had been prominent in the disarmament discussions at the UN, Myrdal as Sweden's top disarmament negotiator and author of widely discussed works on the subject. A member of the upper chamber of parliament, she served in the cabinet for twelve years and was known as the "Grand Old Lady of Swedish Politics." She was married to Gunnar Myrdal, Nobel laureate in economics.

NANSEN, FRIDTJOF (1861–1930). *1922.* Famous Arctic explorer and diplomat of Norway, who directed the refugee programs of the League of Nations and other relief work after World War I.

NOEL-BAKER, PHILIP (1889–1982). *1959.* British Quaker politician and cabinet minister, who played a role in the establishment of both the League of Nations and the United Nations and was a lifelong champion of disarmament.

OFFICE OF THE UNITED NATIONS HIGH COMMISSIONER FOR REFUGEES (1951–   ). *1954.* At the award ceremony Dr. G. JAN VAN HEUVEN GOEDHART of the Netherlands, the High Commissioner, represented his organization, whose work for the uprooted and the homeless, the chairman of the Norwegian Nobel Committee declared, promoted brotherhood among men. See below for the 1981 award.

OFFICE OF THE UNITED NATIONS HIGH COMMISSIONER FOR REFUGEES (1951–   ). *1981.* Accepting the second prize for this agency was its high commissioner, POUL HARTLING of Denmark, who delivered the lecture.

ORBINSKI, JAMES. See Médecins Sans Frontières.

PACHAURI, R. K. See Intergovernmental Panel on Climate Change.

PAULING, LINUS (1901–1994). *1962.* Only winner of two undivided Nobel prizes, one for chemisty and one for peace. Awarded the Peace Prize for his mobilization of the scientists of the world in a protest against nuclear testing in the atmosphere, which helped bring about the partial Test Ban Treaty, concluded in 1963, the year when Pauling received the postponed prize of 1962.

PEARSON, LESTER B. (1897–1972). *1957.* Canadian diplomat and foreign minister, responsible for the establishment of the UN Emergency Force, through which the Suez conflict of 1956 was brought to an end.

PERES, SHIMON (1923–). *1994.* Born in a small Jewish town in White Russia, he emigrated with his family in 1934 to Palestine, where he went to school in an agricultural youth village and then worked on a kibbutz. For two decades he served in the Ministry of Defense in the government of David Ben-Gurion. As a Labor Party leader he held cabinet posts and was prime minister. As foreign minister in the coalition government of YITZHAK RABIN he made an important contribution to the peace agreement with the Palestine Liberation Organization, for which achievement he, YASSER ARAFAT, and Rabin were given the prize.

PÉREZ DE CUÉLLAR, JAVIER. See The United Nations Peace-Keeping Forces.

PÉREZ ESQUIVEL, ADOLFO (1931–). *1980.* A leader in the Latin American nonviolent movement for human rights, who left his position as a teacher of art in Argentina to become the secretary-general of its organization Service for Peace and Justice. Although he was a devout Catholic who opposed acts of violence of the Left as well as of the Right, the military government of Argentina treated him as a subversive and he was subjected to imprisonment and torture.

PIRE, FATHER DOMINIQUE (1910–1969). *1958.* Belgian Dominican priest, who was given the prize "for his efforts to help refugees leave their camps and return to a life of freedom." One project was to build communities of small houses ("villages") next to cities, where the refugees could be integrated in society. Pire was especially concerned with the "Hard Core," the refugees who were old or infirm and often disregarded by other refugee agencies.

PUGWASH CONFERENCES ON SCIENCE AND WORLD AFFAIRS. *1995.* A series of conferences of scientists from many nations to discuss control of nuclear weapons and world security. The first meeting in 1995 in Pugwash, Nova Scotia, was called by Bertrand Russell, Albert Einstein, Frédéric Joliot, and other scientists. Their chief concerns are discussing ways of reducing armaments and examining social responsibilities of scientists. JOHN P. HOLDREN, the Teresa and John Heinz Professor of Environmental Policy and Director of the Program on Science, Technology, and Public Policy in the John F. Kennedy School of Government, and Professor of Environmental Science and Public Policy in the Department of Earth and Planetary Sciences, at Harvard University, served as Chair of the Executive Committee from 1987 to 1997.

RABIN, YITZHAK (1922–1995). *1994.* Born in Jerusalem, he entered upon a military career, rose to chief of staff in 1965, and is given credit for the victory in the Six-Day War of 1967. He next served as ambassador to the United States and on his return turned to politics as a Labor member of the Knesset. He held several cabinet posts and as minister of defense adopted a harsh policy in the effort to suppress the *intifada,* the Palestinian resistance to the occupation. Later, as prime minister again, he decided to work for peace with the Palestinians and authorized SHIMON PERES, his foreign minister, to undertake the secret diplomacy that led to the agreement for which he, Peres, and YASSER ARAFAT were granted the prize. Rabin was assassinated in 1995 by an Israeli fanatic who was opposed to the peace process.

RAMOS-HORTA, JOSÉ. (1949–). *1996.* After the 1975 Indonesian invasion of the tiny Southeast Asian island of East Timor, he became in exile his country's leading spokesman, traveling the globe lobbying world governments for the right of political self-determination for the East Timorese. He persuaded the United Nations to issue several declarations against the Indonesian invasion, and he succeeded in preventing most countries from recognizing Indonesia as a legitimate authority in East Timor.

ROTBLAT, JOSEPH. (1908–2005). *1995.* Polish-born British physicist, international activist against nuclear weapons, cofounder of the PUGWASH CONFERENCES, Rotblat was a member of the Manhattan Project, the group of scientists who designed the first nuclear bomb. He resigned from the project before the bomb was dropped and became an outspoken opponent of nuclear weapons. In 1957 he helped found the Pugwash Conferences on Science and World Affairs, originally organized around the goal of preventing nuclear war, but now also concerned with biological and chemical instruments of mass destruction, as well as the economic and environmental foundations of a durable peace.

SADAT, MOHAMMED ANWAR EL-. See Begin, Menachem.

SAKHAROV, ANDREI (1921–1989). *1975.* Honored by the Nobel Committee as "one of the great champions of human rights in our age," Sakharov was the scientific genius celebrated in the Soviet Union for his role in developing the Soviet hydrogen bomb who became a critic of government policies and courageously asked for liberalization of Soviet society. As the country's leading dissident, Sakharov was persecuted and refused permission to travel to Oslo to receive the prize. But his wife, Yelena Bonner, was already abroad to receive medical treatment and was able to read his acceptance speech and his Nobel lecture at Oslo.

SATO, EISAKU (1901–1975). *1974.* Longtime premier of Japan, he was given the prize after leaving office for his peaceful foreign policy in Asia and for securing Japan's adherence to the nuclear proliferation treaty.

SCHWEITZER, ALBERT (1875–1965). *1952.* Born in the French province of Alsace, recently annexed by the German Empire, Schweitzer was a many-sided genius who could have followed a distinguished career in philosophy, theology, or music, in each of which fields he received a doctorate. Instead, he then trained as a doctor and spent the rest of his life as a medical missionary in the African jungle, putting into practice his convictions about human brotherhood.

SÖDERBLOM, NATHAN (1866–1931). *1930.* As Archbishop of Uppsala and the top prelate of Sweden, he took world leadership in working for peace through the ecumenical movement.

SOYSAL, MÜMTAZ. See Amnesty International.

STRESEMANN, GUSTAV (1878–1929). *1926.* German statesman who, with laureates Aristide Briand of France and Austen Chamberlain of Great Britain, negotiated the treaties of reconciliation among the former enemy states of World War I.

SUTTNER, BERTHA VON (1843–1914). *1905.* The Austrian baroness who wrote the famous antiwar novel *Lay Down Your Arms* and became a major leader of the organized peace movement. She influenced her friend Alfred Nobel in his decision to establish the Peace Prize.

TERESA, MOTHER (1910–1999). *1979.* Known as the "Saint of Calcutta" for her works of mercy for the poor in its slums. Born to an Albanian family in what is now Yugoslav Macedonia, she joined a Catholic teaching order to serve in its missionary school in Calcutta, but overwhelmed by the poverty and misery she found there, she heeded the call to leave the convent and to help the poor while living among them. As she cared for the hungry, the sick, and the dying, others joined her, and she founded a new order, the Missionaries of Charity, whose good works have reached far beyond India to centers of need all over the world.

TRIMBLE, DAVID (1944–). *1998.* Northern Irish politician who played a pivotal role in reaching a landmark agreement in 1998 designed to end three decades of sectarian violence in Northern Ireland. A staunch supporter of the unionist cause, Trimble began his political life as a hard-line opponent of the Ulster Unionists, the mainstream Protestant party that later chose him as leader. His willingness to negotiate with Irish nationalists was politically risky, but the overwhelming approval of the peace accord in May 1998 left him poised to play a prominent role in the new Northern Irish government, if it were to be effectively established.

TUTU, DESMOND MPILO (1931–   ). *1984.* Anglican church leader who was given the prize for his nonviolent struggle against apartheid in South Africa. First a teacher, then an Anglican priest who studied theology in England, Tutu became a bishop and then general secretary of the South African Council of Churches, leading these churches in a campaign against apartheid as contrary to the teachings of Christianity. As the Archbishop of Cape Town, he headed the Anglican Church of South Africa until his retirement in 1996. Then, as Chairman of the Truth and Reconciliation Commission, he made a significant contribution to the healing of his country.

UNITED NATIONS (1945–). *2001.* The prize was jointly awarded to the United Nations and KOFI ANNAN (1938–), a Ghanaian diplomat who served as the seventh UN Secretary-General (1997–2006). The United Nations (UN) is an international organization whose stated aims are to facilitate cooperation in international law, international security, economic development, social progress, and human rights issues. The UN was founded in 1945 to replace the League of Nations, in the hope that it would intervene in conflicts between states and thereby avoid war. Headquartered on international territory within New York City, there are now 192 member states. Secretary-General Annan began his career with the UN in 1962 with the World Health Organization in Geneva; he went on to serve as Under-Secretary-General for Peacekeeping from 1992-96. Secretary-General Annan was considered chiefly responsible for reinvigorating the UN while advancing its peacekeeping and humanitarian efforts, particularly focusing on the battle against HIV/AIDS.

THE UNITED NATIONS PEACE-KEEPING FORCES. *1988.* Accepting the prize for the "Blue Berets" was their commander, JAVIER PÉREZ DE CUÉLLAR, Secretary-General of the United Nations, flanked on either side of the stage by a line of these "soldiers of peace," who had been flown to Oslo for the occasion from their posts around the world. They represented more than ten thousand UN peace-keepers then on duty, stationed as a buffer between hostile forces or monitoring truce agreements. To the chairman of the Nobel Committee the peace-keeping forces, composed of contingents from many countries, were "a tangible expression of the world community's will to solve conflicts by peaceful means."

VAN HEUVEN GOEDHART, DR. G. JAN. See Office of the United Nations High Commissioner for Refugees.

WALESA, LECH (1943–). *1983.* Polish worker who became head of Solidarity, the free trade union movement. The struggle to establish workers' rights and a freer society met with government repression, and Walesa and other leaders were arrested. Although released before the announcement of his prize, Wałesa decided not to go to Oslo, fearing that the government would not permit him to return. He sent his wife, Danuta, to receive the prize, and she read his speech of acceptance. A Solidarity comrade read Wałesa's Nobel lecture, which was then read in Norwegian translation by a well-known actor. He later became president of Poland and served until 1995.

WIESEL, ELIE (1928–). *1986.* Jewish survivor of the Holocaust, born in Romania, now an American citizen. An eloquent author and speaker, honored by the Nobel Committee for his tireless efforts as spokesman for those who died, to keep their memory alive and to defend victims of inhumanity everywhere so that such a tragedy would never happen again. "In him," declared the Nobel Committee chairman, "we see a man who has climbed from utter humiliation to become one of our most important spiritual leaders and guides."

WILLIAMS [PERKINS], BETTY (1943–). *1976.* Cowinner with **MAIREAD MAGUIRE CORRIGAN** (1944–), two young women of simple backgrounds in Belfast, Northern Ireland, who founded the Peace People, a nonviolent movement to reconcile Catholics and Protestants and stop the killing in that troubled province of Great Britain. Williams gave the lecture in behalf of both laureates at the award ceremony in 1977. Both have continued to work for peace: Maguire, with the Peace People in Northern Ireland; Williams, in the United States.

WILLIAMS, JODY (1950–). *1997.* In six years, she and her coworkers made of the ICBL a coalition of more than 1,400 nongovernmental groups, large and small, that persuaded at least ninety national governments to support a total ban on anti-personnel mines.

YUNUS, MUHAMMAD (1940–). *2006.* Awarded jointly to the **GRAMEEN BANK** (1983–) in Bangladesh and its founder, Dr. Muhammad Yunus, "for their efforts to create economic and social development from below." In 1972, Professor Yunus, a Fulbright scholar, became Chair of Economics at the University of Chittagong, but during the national famine in 1974, he became disillusioned with teaching economic theories. The origin of Grameen Bank can be traced back to 1976, when Yunus launched a research project about microcredit to examine the possibility of designing a credit delivery system to provide banking services targeted to the rural poor. He loaned $27 to aid 42 members of a nearby village, and this simple act changed their lives. Yunus went on to found the Grameen Bank in 1983, which currently has 7 million borrowers, mostly women artisans, in 73,000 villages in Bangladesh.

CHRONOLOGY

1901 J. H. Dunant (Switzerland)
F. Passy (France)
1902 E. Ducommun (Switzerland)
C. A. Gobat (Switzerland)
1903 W.R. Cremer (Great Britain)
1904 Institute for Int'l Law, Ghent
(Belgium)
1905 Bertha von Suttner (Austria)
1906 T. Roosevelt (U.S.)
1907 E. T. Moneta (Italy)
L. Renault (France)
1908 K. P. Arnoldson (Sweden)
F. Bajer (Denmark)
1909 A. M. F. Beernaert (Belgium)
P. H. d'Estournelles
de Constant (France)
1910 Int'l Peace Bureau, Bern
(Switzerland)
1911 T. M. C. Asser (Netherlands)
A. H. Fried (Austria)
1912 Elihu Root (U.S.)
1913 H. La Fontaine (Belgium)
1914 None
1915 None
1916 None
1917 Int'l Red Cross, Geneva
1918 None
1919 W. Wilson (U.S.)
1920 L. Bourgeois (France)
1921 K. H. Branting (Sweden)
C. L. Lange (Norway)
1922 F. Nansen (Norway)
1923 None
1924 None
1925 C. G. Dawes (U.S.)
A. Chamberlain (Great
Britain)
1926 A. Briand (France)
G. Stresemann (Germany)
1927 F. Buisson (France)
L. Quidde (Germany)
1928 None
1929 F. B. Kellogg (U.S.)

1930 N. Söderblom
(Sweden)
1931 N. M. Butler (U.S.)
J. Addams (U.S.)
1932 None
1933 N. Angell
(Great Britain)
1934 A. Henderson (Great Britain)
1935 C. von Ossietzky (Germany)
1936 C. Saavedra Lamas
(Argentina)
1937 E. A. R. G. Cecil (Great
Britain)
1938 Nansen Int'l Office for
Refugees, Geneva
1939 None
1940 None
1941 None
1942 None
1943 None
1944 Int'l Committee of the Red
Cross, Geneva
1945 C. Hull (U.S.)
1946 E. G. Balch (U.S.)
J. R. Mott (U.S.)
1947 The Friends Service Council
(Great Britain)
The American Friends Service
Committee (U.S.)
1948 None
1949 J. Boyd-Orr (Great Britain)
1950 R. J. Bunche (U.S.)
1951 L. Jouhaux (France)
1952 A. Schweitzer (France)
1953 G. C. Marshall (U.S.)
1954 Office of the UN High
Commissioner for Refugees,
Geneva
1955 None
1956 None
1957 L. B. Pearson (Canada)
1958 G. H. Pire (Belgium)

1959 P. J. Noel-Baker (Great Britain)
1960 A. J. Lutuli (South Africa)
1961 D. Hammarskjöld (Sweden)
1962 L. C. Pauling (U.S.)
1963 Int'l Committee of the Red Cross, Geneva League of Red Cross Societies, Geneva
1964 M. L. King, Jr. (U.S.)
1965 UN Children's Fund (UNICEF)
1966 None
1967 None
1968 R. Cassin (France)
1969 Int'l Labor Organization, Geneva
1970 N. E. Borlaug (U.S.)
1971 W. Brandt (Germany)
1972 None
1973 H. A. Kissinger (U.S.) [Le Duc Tho (N. Vietnam) (declined the prize)]
1974 S. MacBride (Ireland) E. Sato (Japan)
1975 A. Sakharov (U.S.S.R.)
1976 M. Corrigan (Great Britain) B. Williams (Great Britain)
1977 Amnesty Int'l
1978 M. Begin (Israel) A. Sadat (Egypt)
1979 Mother Teresa (India)
1980 A. Pérez Esquivel (Argentina)
1981 Office of the High Commissioner for Refugees, Geneva
1982 A. Myrdal (Sweden) A. García Robles (Mexico)
1983 L. Wałesa (Poland)
1984 D. Tutu (South Africa)
1985 Int'l Physicians for the Prevention of Nuclear War

1986 E. Wiesel (U.S.)
1987 O. Arias Sánchez (Costa Rica)
1988 UN Peace-Keeping Forces
1989 The Dalai Lama XIV (Tibet)
1990 M. S. Gorbachev (U.S.S.R.)
1991 A. S. Suu Kyi (Myanmar)
1992 R. Menchu Tum (Guatemala)
1993 F. W. de Klerk (South Africa) N. R. Mandela (South Africa)
1994 Y. Arafat (Palestine Liberation Organization) S. Peres (Israel) Y. Rabin (Israel)
1995 Joseph Rotblat (Great Britain) Pugwash Conferences on Science and World Affairs
1996 Carlos Filipe Ximenes Belo (East Timor) José Ramos-Horta (East Timor)
1997 Jody Williams (United States) International Campaign to Ban Landmines
1998 John Hume (Great Britain) David Trimble (Great Britain)
1999 Médecins Sans Frontières (Belgium)
2000 Kim Dae-jung (South Korea)
2001 United Nations Kofi Annan (Ghana)
2002 Jimmy Carter (United States)
2003 Shirin Ebadi (Iran)
2004 Wangari Maathai (Kenya)
2005 International Atomic Energy Agency Mohamed ElBaradei (Egypt)
2006 Muhammad Yunus (Bangladesh) Grameen Bank
2007 Intergovernmental Panel on Climate Change Al Gore, Jr. (United States)

INDEX

About the Editor

IRWIN ABRAMS, Distinguished University Professor Emeritus of Antioch University, is considered the leading authority on the history of the Nobel Peace Prize. He edited the authorized edition of the *Nobel Peace Lectures, 1971–1995*. He has been an advocate for peace his whole life. A Quaker, he participated in the wartime and postwar relief and reconstruction work of the American Friends Service Committee, joint winner of the 1947 Nobel Peace Prize. Professor Abrams is currently revising his award-winning book, *The Nobel Peace Prize and Laureates*. He lives in Yellow Springs, Ohio.

THE ACCLAIMED NEWMARKET *WORDS OF* SERIES

The Words of Albert Schweitzer
Selected and Introduced by Norman Cousins
An inspiring collection focusing on: Knowledge and Discovery, Reverence for Life, Faith, The Life of the Soul, The Musician as Artist, and Civilization and Peace. Includes photographs; chronology; excerpt from acceptance speech for Nobel Peace Prize, 1954; 112 pages.

The Words of Desmond Tutu
Selected and Introduced by Naomi Tutu
Nearly 100 memorable quotations from the addresses, sermons, and writings of South Africa's Nobel Prize–winning archbishop. Topics include: Faith and Responsibility, Apartheid, Family, Violence and Nonviolence, The Community—Black and White, and Toward a New South Africa. Includes photographs; chronology; text of acceptance speech for the Nobel Peace Prize, 1984; 112 pages.

The Words of Gandhi
Selected and with an Introduction by Richard Attenborough
More than 150 selections from the letters, speeches, and writings, collected in five sections—Daily Life, Cooperation, Nonviolence, Faith, and Peace. Includes *TIME* magazine's millennium essay on Gandhi's life and impact on the twentieth century; photographs, chronology, bibliography, glossary; 128 pages.

The Words of Harry S Truman
Selected and Introduced by Robert J. Donovan
This volume of quotations from Truman's speeches and writings gives the essence of his views on politics, leadership, civil rights, war and peace, and "giving 'em hell." Includes photographs, chronology; 112 pages.

The Words of Martin Luther King, Jr.
Selected and Introduced by Coretta Scott King
More than 120 quotations and excerpts from the great civil rights leader's speeches, sermons, and writings on: The Community of Man, Racism, Civil Rights, Justice and Freedom, Faith and Religion, Nonviolence, and Peace. Includes photographs, chronology, text of presidential proclamation of King holiday; 128 pages.

The Words of Peace
Selections from the Speeches of the Winners of the Nobel Peace Prize
Edited by Professor Irwin Abrams. Foreword by President Jimmy Carter.
A new compendium of excerpts from award winners' acceptance speeches spanning 1901 to 2007, including Al Gore, the Dalai Lama, Mother Teresa, Lech Walesa, Martin Luther King, Jr., and Elie Wiesel. Themes are: Peace, Human Rights, Violence and Nonviolence, The Bonds of Humanity, Faith and Hope, plus much more. Includes photographs, biographical notes, chronology and index; 176 pages.

Newmarket Press books are available from your local bookseller or from Newmarket Press, Special Sales Department, 18 East 48th Street, New York, NY 10017; phone 212-832-3575 or 800-669-3903; fax 212-832-3629; e-mail info@newmarketpress.com. Prices and availability are subject to change. Catalogs and information on quantity order discounts are available on request.